An introduction to programming with S-algol

AN INTRODUCTION TO

programming with S-algol

A.J. COLE & R. MORRISON
Department of Computational Science
University of St Andrews

CAMBRIDGE UNIVERSITY PRESS
Cambridge
London New York New Rochelle
Melbourne Sydney

Published by the Press Syndicate of the University of Cambridge
The Pitt Building, Trumpington Street, Cambridge CB2 1RP
32 East 57th Street, New York, NY 10022, USA
296 Beaconsfield Parade, Middle Park, Melbourne 3206, Australia

© Cambridge University Press 1982

First published 1982

Printed in Great Britain at the University Press, Cambridge

Library of Congress catalogue card number: 82-14568

British Library cataloguing in publication data

Cole, A.J.
  An introduction to programming with S-algol.
  1. S-algol (Computer program language)
  I. Title   II. Morrison, R.
  001.64'24   QA76.73.S/

ISBN 0 521 25001 3

CONTENTS

Preface	page vii
1 Simple programs using the **write** clause	1
2 Initialisation and assignment clauses	10
3 The **for** and **while** clauses	19
4 **if** clauses	32
5 Strings	41
6 Vectors	48
7 The **case** clause	59
8 Some important odds and ends	66
9 Procedures	74
10 Structures	87
11 Advanced input and output	98
12 Some complete programming examples	106
13 Backtracking problems	120
14 Outline graphics	134
15 S-algol design philosophy	147
16 S-algol syntax	162
References	167
Appendices	
I S-algol syntax	169
II ASCII codes	173
III List of reserved words	174
IV Standard functions	175
INDEX	179

PREFACE

This book is intended to teach you something about programming in general and something about a new programming language called S-algol (St Andrews Algol) in particular. There is, of course, a lot more to both programming and S-algol than you will find here, but we hope that this will serve as a useful introduction to both. Any new programming language should learn from both the good points and the mistakes of earlier languages and S-algol is no exception. S-algol was first designed and implemented on the PDP 11/40 computer running under the UNIX operating system at the University of St Andrews by Ron Morrison and has been principally influenced by Algol 60 Naur (1963), Algol S Turner & Morrison (1975), Algol W Wirth & Hoare (1966) and BCPL Richards(1969). More recent implementations make S-algol available on the Z80 series of microprocessors running under the CPM operating system and the DEC VAX 11/780 running under VMS. Further details of these implementations can be obtained by writing to the authors of this book.

If you know nothing about programming at all you are probably at an advantage over people who can already program since you have nothing to unlearn. You will, for example, find nothing in this book about flow diagrams or clouds since they are made redundant by the technique developed. The sort of examination question which asks you to find the syntactic errors in a program, which usually arise because of the inadequacies of the language they occur in, is also made redundant. We believe nevertheless that one should learn a discipline of programming, using a language with powerful constructs which can be taught without having to make certain assumptions by faith. Our experience in teaching Algol W and S-algol over the years has convinced us that a well designed language spectacularly reduces the time taken to both write programs and to eliminate errors from them.

You may be concerned about learning a programming language which at the moment is not widely accepted. There are two answers to this. Firstly, the compiler, which is the program which takes your programs and checks them for grammatical mistakes and then converts them into machine code, has been designed with easy transportability from machine to machine in mind. This has already been realised with the exactly compatible implementations on the widely differing architectures of the DEC and Z80 processors and further implementations will follow.

The second reason for learning a good language is that, rather than use outmoded techniques to plan your solution to a problem, you can write your solution in S-algol and then code it in one of the less powerful languages commonly available on other computers. The advantage of this is that you are more likely to get the logic of your solution right first time by this method, thereby avoiding lengthy sessions to find and correct your logical errors.

S-algol is spreading fast. A number of papers Cole & Morrison (1980), Morrison (1982a) and Morrison (1982b) have now appeared on its design and it has been adopted by a number of schools and universities for both teaching and research projects. The language has also been extended to allow graphics Morrison (1982c) and for interval arithmetic Cole & Morrison (1982).

In conclusion we would like to thank our colleagues, both past and present, for their cooperation and criticism in the development and teaching of new languages at St Andrews. In particular we would like to thank David Turner with whom the design of S-algol started and who will recognise that the language contains a number of his ideas. Tony Davie also contributed to the design of S-algol as did Pete Bailey who now maintains the system and Paul Maritz who implemented the Z80 version. Tony and Pete undertook the task of proof reading this book and made numerous suggestions and improvements. We cannot thank them enough for their contribution.

We hope that you enjoy reading this book and will be extremely grateful for your criticisms - we do not guarantee to take any notice of them but we will certainly enthusiastically discuss any points that you raise either in connection with the language itself or the way in which it has been presented here.

1 SIMPLE PROGRAMS USING THE WRITE CLAUSE

Writing correct programs is a lot simpler if you use a good programming language. To show you how easy it can be in S-algol we will write our first complete program straight away.

write "This is an S-algol program." ?

The effect of this program is to print out the line of text

This is an S-algol program.

Although it must be admitted that this is not very exciting, there are a lot of things about S-algol programming that we can learn from it. First of all the word **write** is a command to the computer to print out the value of the expression (or, as we shall see shortly, perhaps the values of a list of expressions) that follows it. In this case the expression to be printed is

"This is an S-algol program."

This particular expression is an example of a string literal. A string is one of the types of data we can use and manipulate in an S-algol program. A string literal is a particularly simple sort of expression being just an ordered collection of characters including spaces and punctuation marks and indeed almost any other character you can type from your keyboard. A string literal must always be written in quotes as shown above. This is to enable the compiler to distinguish it from other types of literal which we do not wish to regard as strings.

Thus, for example, 156 is an integer literal but "156" is a string literal. The reason for making this distinction will become clear later. If you want to include a quotation mark " inside a string this causes a slight problem, since it will be mistaken for the end of the string. We overcome this difficulty by writing an apostrophe followed by a quotation mark '" side by side if we want the quotation mark inside the string. The apostrophe is a special symbol as we shall see later. If you want to use an apostrophe itself in a string you must type '', that is, two apostrophes, side by side.

The S-algol compiler always evaluates expressions following the **write** command before printing them. The resulting value of a string literal is particularly simple being just the string itself. The quotation marks are stripped off by the compiler when the program is read into the computer. This explains why the output from the program is

This is an S-algol program.
rather than
"This is an S-algol program."

The question mark at the end of the program should always be present at the end of any program. It is there to indicate to the S-algol compiler that there is no more program to follow. This does not prevent you from using the question mark as part of a string literal if you wish since S-algol does not look in detail at the characters inside a string but just regards the whole string as a collection of characters. This indeed is another reason why a string literal must always be enclosed in quotes so that no attempt is made to analyse its internal meaning.

One final point about our first program. The word **write** has been printed in bold type. This is to emphasise that it is a special word that has a known meaning in S-algol. Such a word is called a reserved word and is one of a whole list of reserved words that you will learn in the rest of this book. We will always print reserved words in bold type in programs in this book since this draws attention to them and makes the program easier to read. When you write programs it is good practice to underline reserved words in your written copy. However when you type reserved words into the computer leave out the underlining since it is very tedious to have to type so much. Indeed underlining will be treated as an error.

For our second example we will take

write 3 * 2 + 5 - 7 ?

The spaces are optional and the computer will respond by printing

The reason for this is that the expression following the **write** command is an integer expression and this is evaluated before printing the result. The asterisk '*' indicates multiplication and is used to avoid confusion between the usual multiplication sign and the letter x. This is common practice in computing and is a consequence of poor printing facilities on early computers which had no multiplication sign. Note that if we had written

write "3 * 2 + 5 - 7" ?

the computer would have responded by printing

    3 * 2 + 5 - 7

since we would be asking it to print a string literal.

We mentioned before that we could follow the **write** command with a list of expressions. To form such a list we simply write down the expressions separated by commas. It should now be obvious that the program

write 3 + 4 - 9,3 * 2 + 5 ?

will produce the output

    -2   11

since the list contains the two expressions 3 + 4 - 9 and 3 * 2 + 5 both of which are evaluated separately before printing.

It is not necessary for each of the expressions in a list to be of the same type. It is good programming practice to make your results as readable as possible. Thus we could write the program

write "3 + 2 * 6 = ",3 + 2 * 6 ?

giving the output

    3 + 2 * 6 = 15

since the first expression is a string literal and the second an integer expression. You may have started wondering if the answer to the above example is 15 or 30 depending on the order in which you do the arithmetic. For the moment we will say that the order is the same as you would do it in ordinary arithmetic but we will come back to this point in a later chapter. In the meantime if you are in any doubt you can use brackets to make the meaning clear. Thus

(3 * 2) + (4 * 4)

has the same value as

3 * 2 + 4 * 4

but not the same as

3 * (2 + 4) * 4

As another example of mixing expressions consider the program

write "The square of 27 is",27 * 27," and its cube is ",27 * 27 * 27,"." ?

You should now understand why the result printed is

The square of 27 is 729 and its cube is 19683.

We do not have to stick to integers in doing arithmetic. If we write

write (7.8 * 9.2 + 3.6) / 1.2 ?

we will obtain the result

62.8

We have used here the division sign in computing which is the oblique stroke /. The numbers used, all of which have a decimal point in them, are called real numbers to distinguish them from the integers which do not have a decimal point but only an implied one after their rightmost digit. Thus

187

is an integer according to the definition but

187.0 and 187.

are both real numbers. A real number must always start with a digit. Thus the fraction 1/2 must be written as 0.5 and not just .5.

You are allowed to mix integers and real numbers in an

expression but if you do the answer will always be given as a real number. Thus

write 5 * 27 / 1.2 ?

will give the result

      112.5

and

write 6 * 27 / 1.2 ?

will give the result

      135.0

When we spoke about integer arithmetic earlier on, we deliberately avoided using the division operator because it is not always obvious what the result should be. If we divide 4 by 2 then the answer is 2 but if we divide 5 by 2 then the exact answer is 2.5 if we are working in real arithmetic, or 2 with remainder 1 if we are working in integers. Computers are stupid things and we have to make clear distinctions in cases like this to be quite clear what we mean. To be fair to computers, some human beings have the same problem!

We make the situation unambiguous by insisting that the division operation, when we use /, will always have a real result. Thus

      7 / 2

will have the result

      3.5

and

      6 / 2

will have the result

      3.0

both answers being real numbers. Recognising that sometimes we do want to do integer arithmetic with integer answers we introduce two new operators **div** and **rem** which work as follows

      9 **div** 4

gives the integer result

> 2

which is the integer result of dividing 9 by 2 and

> 9 **rem** 4

gives the integer result

> 1

that is, the remainder on division of 9 by 4. These new operators can be used in integer expressions in exactly the same way as the other arithmetic operators. Note that both **div** and **rem** are reserved words.

The following example uses **div** and **rem** to convert a given number of days to the corresponding number of weeks and days.

write 278," days is ",278 **div** 7," weeks and ",278 **rem** 7," days." ?

will output

> 278 days is 39 weeks and 5 days.

To finish off this chapter we will give one more example of a **write** clause using a string literal. The program

write
"   Mary had a little lamb,
          Its fleece as black as soot,
          And everywhere that Mary went,
          Its sooty foot it put." ?

will produce the output

> Mary had a little lamb,
> Its fleece as black as soot,
> And everywhere that Mary went,
> Its sooty foot it put.

The poem is spaced out in lines like this because when the program is typed at a computer terminal, a key giving a new line has to be pressed and an internal character corresponding to this new line is stored away with the string itself. Note also that in order to place the output nearer to the centre of the page, the opening quote was put over at the left margin. This took up one character itself so, to give the same number of spaces before each line in the actual output, we put the opening M one space further across in the first line. We could have avoided this particular difficulty by typing the initial quote followed by a new line immediately but this would have left an extra blank line before the first line of the poem.

In all the previous examples the output generated by different expressions in a list continued on the same line. To give the user fuller control over the layout of output on the printed page we introduce a new print line convention. In addition to being able to get new lines as in the above example you can also get a new line by typing 'n, that is, the apostrophe character followed by an n, as part of any string literal in the **write** clause. To illustrate this point consider the program

write 3 + 2,5 * 7 ?

with output

      5   35

If we had written it as

write 3 + 2,"'n",5 * 7 ?

the output would have been

      5
     35

At this stage in learning to program this probably seems a clumsy way to control output but we will see later that it is part of a powerful and flexible system.

Exercises 1

1.1 Write a program to print your name and address as you would write it on an envelope.

1.2 Write a program to convert 584 ounces into pounds and ounces. Your output should not just be two numbers but a statement that the given number of ounces is equal to so many pounds and so many ounces.

1.3 In this chapter you have learned three reserved words. What is meant by a reserved word and what are the three reserved words you have learned.

1.4 The expressions you have learned so far are of type string, integer and real. What are the types of the following expressions and what are their values?

    (i)   3 + 2 * 6
    (ii) "3 + 2 * 6"
    (iii) 5.4 * 6.4 + 2.3 * 3.7
    (iv) 8 **div** 3 + 15 **rem** 6
    (v)   6 + 8 / 2
    (vi) (-9) **div** 2

1.5 Write a program to print on two lines the statements

    The square of 24 is 576
    The square of 31 is 961

Your program should only use the word **write** once and should calculate the two squares itself.

Solutions to Exercises 1

1.1
write "   Professor A.J.Cole,
              '"Inisheer'",
              Barnyards,
              Kilconquhar,
              FIFE." ?

Note the apostrophe, quote symbols around the name of the house appear in the output as single quotes. Why has the name of the professor not been written above the address? How could you overcome this easily? (See "Mary had a little lamb").

1.2
write 584," ounces is equal to ",584 **div** 16,"pounds and ",
      584 **rem** 16," ounces" ?

Note that although that we have run over to a new line in writing the program, the output will all appear on the same line since there are no new line symbols inside the string literals and we have not used the 'n symbol. The output will be

        584 ounces is equal to 36 pounds and 8 ounces

1.3 A reserved word is a word which has a special meaning in the S-algol language. Reserved words must only be used in a program when they have the intended meaning unless they happen to be part of a string literal when their fixed meaning is ignored. The three reserved words we have met so far are **write, div** and **rem**.

1.4   (i)   type integer, value 15
- (ii) type string, value "3 + 2 * 6"
- (iii) type real, value 43.07
- (iv) type integer, value 5. Note that 8 **div** 3 has value 2 and 15 **rem** 6 has value 3.
- (v)   type real, value 10.0. Note that 8/2 is of type real since the operation is real division. It makes no difference that 2 happens to divide 8 exactly.
- (vi) type integer, value -4. This one is a bit unfair since we did not talk about integer division with negative numbers. The rule is as follows. Forget about the signs and apply **div** as if both numbers were positive. Then if exactly one of the two numbers is negative make the answer negative. Note that
x **rem** y is always x - y * (x **div** y).

1.5
write "The square of 24 is ",24 * 24,"'nThe square of 31 is ",31 * 31 ?

Note that the new line symbol 'n appears inside the quotes.

2 INITIALISATION AND ASSIGNMENT CLAUSES

In Chapter 1, whenever we used a number or a string we had to write it explicitly in the program. This meant that whenever we wanted to repeat the calculation with different numbers or strings we had to rewrite the whole program. The main reason for using a computer is to save time and effort and one way of doing this is to write programs which will work for many different sets of data. For example, in the program which worked out the square and cube of 27, the program would be more useful if, instead of just working with the number 27, it could be modified to 'read' an integer and then calculate its square and cube. Thus the same program could be used to calculate the squares and cubes of many different integers. The following S-algol program will do this for us.

let X = **readi**
write "The square of ",X," is ",X * X," and its cube is ",X * X * X ?

The clauses in this program need some explanation but first we will give a general idea of how it works. The program first 'reads' an integer which is supplied by the user and makes this the value of the object called X. You can think of X as being the name of a pigeon-hole inside the machine and the user writes an integer, say 30, on a piece of paper and pops it in the pigeon-hole. X is then the name of the pigeon-hole and 30 is the value of X. The effect of evaluating the very simple expression X in the **write** clause list is to find its value which is 30. Similarly X * X works out 30 * 30 and gives the answer 900 and X * X * X gives 27000. The effect of the whole program given 30 as data is to print

The square of 30 is 900 and its cube is 27000

The clause

let X = **readi**

is an example of an initialising declaration and introduces four very important ideas.

(i) The reserved word **let** is used to indicate that the name of a new object is to follow, in this case the name is X. Every time we want to use a new name for an object in our program we do it in this way. Some primitive programming languages allow you to use names without specifically declaring them in this way, but although this may be easy to start with, it can cause a lot of trouble later.

(ii) The **readi** part of the clause causes the computer to 'get' an integer from somewhere. For the moment we will suppose that 'get' means that the computer waits for the user, that is you, to type in an integer from the terminal when the program is running. There are many other ways in which the computer can 'get' an integer but we will leave these for the present. If, by the way, you do not type an integer here but perhaps type a string, S-algol will tell you that you have made a mistake in the data and stop running your program.

(iii) The = part of the clause does two things. It puts a copy of the integer you have just supplied into the pigeon-hole named X and tells the system that this is a constant and must not be changed in your program during execution. S-algol will keep an eye on it and if you try to alter the value of X in the rest of your program it will print you an error message at compilation time. Although this may seem tedious to the beginner it is of great help in avoiding errors when you come to write more complex programs.

(iv) The fact that we have written **readi** ensures that the number to be read is an integer. It also tells S-algol that X is to hold an integer and this information is also remembered by the compiler and can be used to detect subsequent errors in your program.

You should now go back and read the above program again and make sure that you understand what it does.

In addition to the **readi** clause we also have **readr** and **reads** clauses which as you may guess read a real number and a string respectively. Thus

      let Y = **reads**

will read a string and assign it to Y which will now have the type string attached to it and similarly for **readr**.

Data supplied by the user at execution time must satisfy the same syntactic conditions as literals included as parts of programs as discussed in Chapter 1. In particular, string literals must be enclosed in quotes, integers do not have a decimal point and reals may be either in the format described in Chapter 1 or may be given as integers which will be converted into real numbers internally. Successive reals or integers must be separated either by spaces or by appearing on a new line. The condition that string literals must be enclosed in quotes may seem a nuisance to the beginner but the reason for it is to keep to a minimum the conditions to be imposed on the way in which string literals can be written. We will discuss later how to remove this condition when you have learnt more about programming and when you know more about the sort of data that may be supplied to a particular program.

Initialising declarations do not necessarily have a read command on their right hand side. Any expression can be written. So

      let N = 1

makes the object of name N an integer constant with value 1 and

      let P = 3.0 * 6.5 + 4.3

makes P a real constant with value 23.8. Note that S-algol is clever enough to deduce the type of an expression without you having to tell it.

Expressions can involve previously declared objects as well as literals. You can declare these yourself or as in the following example use one such as pi which is predeclared by S-algol itself.

let radius = **readr**
let area = pi * radius * radius
let circumference = 2.0 * pi * radius
write "The area of a circle of radius ",radius," is ",area,
     "´nand its circumference is ",circumference,".´n" ?

If the value 2.6 is given to radius then the result will be

>The area of a circle with radius 2.6 is 21.2372
>and its circumference is 16.3363.

You can use as many letters as you like for the name of an object. You may also use integers and the full stop character provided that you always start the name with a letter. Thus

>average
>K9
>father.christmas

are all valid object names. On the other hand

>14B

is not since it does not start with a letter and

>santa claus

is not since it has a space in the middle. (santa.claus is of course valid). It is good programming practice to give names to objects which indicate their use since it makes the program easier to read and understand. This is why you are allowed to use the full stop and you can use names like

>lower.limit

or

>pupil.name

All the above declarations introduce names which are to be used and make them constant. We also need to use variables whose value can change during the execution of a program. This is possible using a slightly different declarative clause. For example

>**let** count := 0

declares the variable with name count to be an integer with initial value 0. The combination of characters := is used in place of = to indicate that count is a variable whose value can be changed later. Once the variable's name has been declared in a **let** clause, subsequent clauses which change its value are written without the **let**. For example

```
        count := count + 1
```

This clause may be read as 'count becomes count plus one' and the meaning is always, evaluate the right hand side and assign the new value to the variable named on the left. The clause above thus adds one to the current value of the variable count. S-algol will check for you that the type of the expression on the right is the same as that of the identifier on the left and will give an error message if it is not. To the beginner this may seem an added and unnecessary complication but the reason is again to enable S-algol to help you avoid obscure errors in more complicated programs you may write later on. The one exception to this rule is that integer expressions may be assigned to real variables in which case their values are automatically changed to real for you.

We will now give some examples of the use of these ideas. The first example is to print the value of an expression which uses a complicated factor several times.

```
let Q = 1.73 + 4.2 * 0.73
write 5.69 / ( 2 * Q ) + 4.16 / ( ( 3 * Q - 7.77 ) / ( 4 * Q ) ) ?
```

Note that S-algol sorts out the mixture of reals and integers and prints the answer as a real.

Next we print out the square and the cube of a number by a method different from that above.

```
let X = readr
let Y := X * X
write "The square of ",X," is ",Y
Y := Y * X
write " and its cube is ",Y,"'n" ?
```

In this case X is a real constant with a value that is read in, say 3.86. Y is declared to be a variable of type real with its first value being X squared. The first **write** clause produces the output

        The square of 3.86 is 14.8996

Y is then given a new value which is the old value times X. That is, the new value of Y is X cubed and the second **write** clause prints

        and its cube is 57.512456

on the same line as the first since we have not used a new line symbol in either clause. This is rather a clumsy way of solving the problem since the program

let X = **readr**
write "The square of ",X," is ",X * X," and its cube is ",X * X * X ?

would do the same thing. However, the example shows that X is a constant and Y is a variable in the program.

    It is useful to put comments into a program to help explain to the reader what is being done but which are not really part of the program itself. In S-algol this is very easy. We use the exclamation mark symbol ! to indicate that anything following it on the same line is a comment and should be ignored by the S-algol compiler. It is good practice to put a comment at the start of each program giving your name and what the program is intended to do. For example, we could write a program to convert money in sterling to francs and lire reading in the sum of money we wish to convert and the exchange rates from British to French and Italian currency as follows.

!Joe Bloggs. Conversion from sterling to francs and lire
!Data is a value in pounds and pence written as one decimal
!e.g. 28.18, and the current conversion rates for francs and lire
let sterling.value = **readr**
let franc.rate = **readr** ; **let** lire.rate = **readr**
write sterling.value," pounds convert to ",sterling.value * franc.rate,
    " francs and ",sterling.value * lire.rate," lire'n" ?

    We have slipped in a new idea here. We have put two clauses on one line and separated them by a semi-colon. You can separate clauses in this way anywhere you like in your program if you feel that it makes it easier to understand.

    If you are a beginner this is probably the most difficult chapter to understand in the book. If you have had any difficulty go back and read it again. If you still do not fully understand it do not despair. Read it again after the next few chapters.

Exercises 2

2.1 Write down initialising declarations for the following
    (i) An integer variable P with value 6.
    (ii) A real constant Q with value 3.68 * R + 2.2.
    (iii) A string constant with value "Yes".

2.2 What is the type of the name T in each of the following clauses. Indicate also whether it is constant or variable.
    (i) **let** T = 59 **div** 13
    (ii) **let** T := **reads**
    (iii) T := 5 + 7 / 3
    (iv) **let** T = "1.4"

2.3 Write a program to convert a temperature in degrees fahrenheit to degrees centigrade. Your program should read the number of degrees fahrenheit as a real number. Include comments to say what you are doing and use meaningful names.

2.4 Write a program to work out the value of pi squared using the value of pi given by S-algol. Also work out the number 22/7 and write out its value and its difference from the value of pi given. Do the same thing for pi squared and 22/7 squared putting your answer on a new line. You should include comments on what you are doing and also include string literals in your **write** clause to make the whole output understandable without reading your program.

2.5 A simplified tax system computes the tax due on the income for a given person by first computing the taxable income by subtracting the personal allowance and child allowance for each child from the income. The tax due is then equal to the current tax rate times the taxable income. The nett income is equal to the income minus the tax due. Assuming that the child allowance is $500 per child and the tax rate is 28% write a program to read in, for one individual, the salary, personal allowance and number of children and to print out the income, taxable income, tax due and nett income. Both your program and your output should be self-explanatory.

Solutions to Exercises 2

2.1   (i)   **let** P := 6
       (ii)   **let** Q = 3.68 * R + 2.2
       (iii)   **let** S = "Yes"

2.2   (i)   integer constant
       (ii)   string variable
       (iii)   real variable. Remember that a / b is real
       (iv)   string constant

2.3
!Jack Cole. Convert from fahrenheit to centigrade.
let fahrenheit = **readr**
write fahrenheit," degrees fahrenheit converts to ",
     (fahrenheit - 32) * 5 / 9," degrees centigrade´n" ?

2.4
!Jack Cole. Comparison of pi with 22 / 7
!and the comparison of the corresponding squares.
let pi.approx = 22 / 7
write "The value of pi is ",pi,
"´nand the value of 22 / 7 is ",pi.approx,
"´n and their difference is ", pi - pi.approx,
"´n The value of pi squared is ",pi * pi,
"´n and the value of 22 / 7 squared is ",pi.approx * pi.approx,
"´n and their difference is ",
pi * pi - pi.approx * pi.approx,"´n" ?

        Note that it might have been better to introduce two new constants by

let pi.sq = pi * pi
let pi.approx.sq = pi.approx * pi.approx

and to have used these values directly in the **write** clause. Rewrite the program using this idea.

2.5
```
!Jack Cole.  Program to compute tax etc.
let child.allowance = 500       !More readable than writing
let tax.rate = 0.28             !500 and 0.28 in the program.
let income = readr
let allowance = readr
let no.of.children = readi
let taxable.income = income - allowance -
                         no.of.children * child.allowance
let tax.due = taxable.income * tax.rate
write "Income",income,
      "'nTaxable income",taxable.income,
      "'nTax due",tax.due,
      "'nNett income",income - tax.due,"'n" ?
```

Note that you have not yet learnt how to test for a negative taxable income. We will show you how to do this in Chapter 4 so we will assume for the moment that the data supplied is compatible with the method of solution! You will also learn how to control the layout of real numbers in a **write** clause in Chapter 8.

3   THE FOR AND WHILE CLAUSES

The programs we have written so far have been simple lists of clauses with each clause being executed once only. Computers are particularly good at doing repetitive tasks and we write programs to make use of this fact. Since many problems can be solved in this way, we introduce some special clauses to help in making the computer repeat sequences of clauses.

Most programming languages have a **for** clause and S-algol is no exception. The following program works out factorial n. Factorial n is defined as $n*(n-1)*....*2*1$ for a given n.

```
!J.Cole. Factorial program
let n = readi ; let factorial := 1
for i = 2 to n do
   factorial := i * factorial
write "factorial ",n," is ",factorial,"'n" ?
```

There are three new reserved words used here, namely **for**, **to** and **do**. The **for** clause does several things. Firstly it declares a new integer 'i'. This integer 'i' is initially set to 2 and the clause following **do** is executed provided that $n \geq 2$. The effect of the clause following **do** is to multiply 1 by 2 and put the result in factorial. The computation then goes back to the start of the **for** clause and adds 1 to 'i' making its new value 3, tests this against n and if $i \leq n$ repeats execution of the clause following **do** making the new value of factorial equal to 6. It continues in this way until, for the first time, the new value of 'i' exceeds the value of n. At this point it skips over the clause following **do** and continues with the **write** clause. Notice we have put the clause factorial := i * factorial

a little across the page. S-algol ignores spaces so we can write our
programs like this to make them more readable. The way we have written out
the program emphasises the fact that this clause is the one 'controlled'
by the **for** clause. You should get into the habit of laying out your
programs so that they are readable. Keep an eye on how it is done in this
book and try to copy the ideas.

There are several points to note about the **for** clause. The
name 'i' used above can be replaced by any other name we wish to use. To
be consistent with our earlier notation for assignment we have used =
rather than := in the **for** clause. At first sight this appears to be a
contradiction since 'i' takes successive values 2,3,... and in this sense
is not a constant. However the logical interpretation is that each time
the computation returns to the **for** part of the clause it defines a new
constant 'i' with the incremented value. The important thing is that 'i'
is a constant in the clause controlled by the **for** clause and cannot be
changed by programmed assignment. This is good programming practice since
even experienced programmers find logical difficulty in using **for** clauses
in languages which allow internal assignment to the control variable. If
you really want to program this way you can do it by using the **while**
clause to be described later in this chapter but the effect will be
entirely your own responsibility. Note that 'i' only exists while the **for**
clause is being executed. If we tried to print 'i' instead of n in the
write clause we would be told that it no longer existed.

The numbers 2 and n used in the above **for** clause are simple
examples of integer expressions. You can use any integer expressions you
please in **for** clauses. The value of 'i' is set initially to the value of
the first expression and the limit for 'i' is set to the second.

The above form of the **for** loop always counts in 1's. If we
wished to count in 2's say, we could modify the clause to

    for i = 1 **to** n **by** 2 **do**

The new reserved word **by** tells S-algol that the count is to be
done in steps of 2 (in this case). More generally we can put any integer
expression in place of 2.

It would be very restrictive to allow only one clause as
written above to be controlled by the **for** clause. If we want to execute

several clauses we can do this by taking a sequence of clauses and surrounding them with braces { and } or by the reserved words **begin** and **end**. For small sequences of clauses it is probably clearer to use braces. The sequence of clauses is a very important concept in S-algol and although the sequence contains several clauses inside itself, it is regarded as a single clause. We regard a complete S-algol program as a sequence of clauses in this sense.

The following example illustrates the use of a sequence controlled by a **for** clause.

```
!J.Cole. Program to print a shopping list and total cost.
write "Shopping list'n"          !This gives a heading to the output
let total := 0.0                 !This initialises the total cost to zero
let no.of.items = readi          !This gets the total number of items
for I = 1 to no.of.items do
begin
    let quantity = readi ; let name = reads ; let cost.per.item = readr
    let line.total = quantity * cost.per.item
    total := total + line.total
    write quantity,name," at ",cost.per.item,line.total,"'n"
end                              !Notice the program layout
write "Total cost of bill is ",total,"'n" ?
```

The meaning of this program should be obvious. Note that the only variable in the program is 'total'. Although 'quantity', 'name' and 'cost.per.item' all change their value, they remain constant during any one particular execution of the sequence of clauses. Because the word **let** is inside the sequence for each of the items, they are redefined as new constants each time the sequence is repeated. On the other hand, 'total' is declared outside the sequence since we want to set it to zero initially, accumulate its value and then eventually print it out **after** all the items have been read in and added to the list.

A suitable data set for this program could be

```
6
2  " lbs of sugar"    0.16
1  " lb of butter"    0.60
```

```
6  " oranges      "    0.10
3  " bottle coke  "    0.27
1  " tin pears    "    0.48
6  "boxes matches"     0.03
```

Note that the items may be separated by either a new line or at least one space. By writing out the data as we have done, we ensure that the strings all have the same length by padding them out with spaces, so we will get a nice neat layout for our bill. We will describe more elegant ways of doing this later on.

We could have used braces here instead of the words **begin** and **end** but it is clearer not to. It is probably better to save the braces for use when all the clauses in the sequence can be put on the **same line**.

To avoid confusion in the future we need to introduce briefly a new idea, namely that of the 'scope' of an object. As we have seen in the above example we can declare new objects by initialisation clauses anywhere we like in the program. However, if we define a new object in a particular sequence of clauses that object only remains in existence at execution time from the point of its declaration to the end of the sequence. This is called the scope of the object. The moment we leave the sequence, that is, execute another clause outwith the sequence, then all the objects declared inside the sequence are no longer in scope. If after leaving the sequence we enter it again a new 'instance' of the object is created and this has no recollection of previous instances.

Declaring 'total' in the program above as a variable in the outer sequence allows us to accumulate a running total each time we enter the inner sequence. None of the other information in the inner sequence is required in the long term so it can be safely declared there and does not remain in existence to cause possible trouble later. Note also that although, for example, 'quantity' may well be given a different value each time we enter the sequence in which it is declared, that value remains constant during the current execution of the sequence. It can and should be declared using '=' rather than ':='. It would not be wrong to use ':=' but it is better programming practice to recognise which objects are constant and which are variables and to declare them accordingly.

This discussion of scope should help to clarify the argument for regarding the control identifier in a **for** loop as a constant rather than a variable.

One final point about scope. If we declare an object in an inner sequence with the same name as one in an outer sequence then the existence of the outer object is temporarily suspended and a new object with the same name is created. On leaving the inner sequence this new object is discarded and the old one reinstated along with its suspended value. This facility is not of much use to the beginner but is very useful when programs are being written jointly by several people, so that someone writing an inner sequence does not have to be told and have to check the name of every object in the outer sequence so as to avoid using these names twice with different meanings.

The **while** clause gives us an alternative way of constructing a repetitive part of a program. We begin by rewriting the first example using the **while** clause.

```
!J.Cole. Alternative factorial program.
let n = readi ; let factorial := 1 ; let I := 2
while I ≤ n do { factorial := I * factorial ; I := I + 1 }
write "factorial ",n," is ",factorial,"´n" ?
```

The way in which the **while** clause works is that the condition which follows the word **while** is evaluated. The answer could be **true** or **false**. If it is **true** then the clause following **do** is evaluated and then the condition is evaluated again. So long as the condition remains **true** this process is repeated but as soon as the condition becomes **false** the program jumps over the clause following **do** and continues with the next part of the program. Try following through the action of this program with n being given a value 5 say.

We have talked about the condition following the word **while**. It would have been more accurate to have referred to this as a boolean expression. A boolean expression is an expression which evaluates to one of two values **true** or **false**. The particular example that we have given namely I ≤ n is either **true** or **false** at any particular instant in time. We will see later on that we can write quite complicated boolean expressions and any such one will do to control a **while** loop.

Notice that one of the clauses in curly brackets changes one of the variables in the condition. If this were not the case the boolean value of the condition would never change and the looping operation would go on for ever.

This particular example makes the programming slightly more difficult than the previous one using the **for** clause. However, there are many cases in which we cannot replace the **while** clause by an equivalent **for** loop. To show the full power of the **while** loop we really need some more examples but we will illustrate the point with the shopping list program above. One very artificial thing that we did in the example was to count the number of items in our list and give that number as the first piece of data. This was necessary so that we could set up the count for the **for** loop. We will eliminate the need to count the number of data items, making the computer do it for us, by adding one extra row to our shopping list data with a value that cannot possibly occur. For example we will never want to include a line for zero articles, so we set up the data as follows

```
         2    "lbs of sugar "      0.16
         1    "lb of butter "      0.60
         6    "oranges       "     0.10
         3    "bottle coke   "     0.27
         1    "tin pears     "     0.48
         6    "boxes matches"      0.03
         0
```

and we write our program using the **while** clause.

```
write "Shopping list'n"
let total := 0.0 ; let quantity := readi
while quantity ≠ 0 do
begin
     let name = reads ; let cost.per.item = readr
     let line.total = quantity * cost.per.item
     total := total + line.total
     write quantity,name," at ",cost.per.item,line.total,"'n"
     quantity := readi         !This is where we change the condition
end
write "Total cost of bill is ",total,"'n" ?
```

Notice that the program starts by reading the integer 2 at the start of the first line. The test is to see if 2 is not equal to 0 and this is **true**. We proceed to read the other two items on the line and continue with the calculations as before. Finally, the last clause reads the first integer on the next line and then goes back to test the condition

$$\text{quantity} \neq 0$$

again. It continues to repeat this operation until it finally reads 0 and at this stage the condition $0 \neq 0$ is **false** and for the first time we jump out of the loop and finish off the program. Notice also that by being cunning and putting the second two read clauses inside the sequence at the beginning we only have to put a single 0 on the last line and not a whole line of redundant data.

An even better way to terminate the input of data for this problem requires another programming concept, namely that of the file. In most computer systems it is possible to record collections of information in files and to refer to these files by their names. In particular your terminal is regarded as a file and you supply the information for the file from the keyboard. Other files in the system have a predefined fixed amount of information in them and are always terminated by an end of file (eof). On your terminal there will be some combination of keys (e.g. control z) which signifies that no more information is to be supplied from that source. You will need to consult your operating system manuals to find the particular eof symbols for your terminal. Once you have terminated input in this way you need special techniques, which we will not discuss here, to continue input again. However, in our example, we do not need to put in any more data after the end of our shopping list so, instead of a single 0 as above we can terminate our input with eof. We can now use ~**eof** as the boolean expression controlling our **while** loop. The ~ symbol means boolean negation. That is, if **eof** is **false** then ~**eof** is **true** and therefore ~**eof** will not terminate the execution of the loop until input ceases with eof. This also avoids the clumsiness of having to declare 'quantity' outside the loop and then to alter its value at the end of the clause controlled by the **while** loop. Furthermore, 'quantity' becomes a constant rather than a variable. The complete program is now

```
write "Shopping list´n"
let total := 0.0
while ~eof do
begin
    let quantity = readi ; let name = reads ; let cost.per.item = readr
    let line.total = quantity * cost.per.item
    total := total + line.total
    write quantity,name," at ",cost.per.item,line.total,"´n"
end
write "Total cost of bill is ",total,"´n" ?
```

The **while** clause as described above has its test for execution before any of the code in the controlled clause. This means that whenever the test fails, including possibly the first time that the test is made, the controlled clause is skipped over. Thus the controlled text can be executed zero or many times. It is useful to have another construct which tests after the execution of the controlled clause, thus ensuring that the controlled clause is executed at least once.

The **repeat** construct enables us to do this. For example

```
repeat x := 0.5 * ( x + a/x )
while rabs( x - a/x ) > 0.000001
```

This piece of program assumes that x has been initialised to some suitable starting value and then applies the Newton iterative square root calculating formula until the condition is satisfied. The calculation for a new x is carried out at least once. A function rabs has been used here. It calculates the absolute value of the real number which is its argument. A corresponding function abs calculates the absolute value of its integer argument. We will see later that functions are a very important and powerful programming mechanism that we will make good use of. It is tedious to have to write out very small or very large constants in full. To alleviate this problem we use the notation 1.0e-6 to indicate that 1.0 is to be multiplied by 10 raised to the power -6. We could have written the constant 0.000001 in this way.

As another example, consider the following program segment to calculate factorial n where n is assumed to have been assigned an integer

```
value > 1

let factorial := 1 ; let i := 2
repeat { factorial := factorial * i ; i := i + 1 }
while i ≤ n
```

  A third variation on the position of the test condition in this construction would be for it to appear in the middle of the controlled clause rather than at the beginning or end. This can be done with a combination of the **repeat** and **while** constructs. As an example, consider the problem of reading a large number of positive real numbers in order to find their how many there are, their sum and the sum of their squares. Very often we don't know how many numbers there are and there is no point in counting them if we have a computer to do it for us. In some cases where information is being gathered as the computation proceeds we may not even know how many pieces of data there are going to be. In our case we have assumed that all the data is positive so we will arbitrarily terminate our data with a zero which is not to be counted as a real data item. You can almost always choose some impractical value as a terminator for the data in practical problems as we did in the second attempt at the shopping list example.

  A program sequence to carry out the above calculation would be

```
let number := 0 ; let sum := 0.0
let sum.sq := 0.0 ; let item := 0.0
repeat item := readr
while item > 0 do
begin
     number := number + 1
     sum := sum + item
     sum.sq := sum.sq + item * item
end
```

  Here the test takes place after each new item has been read and so long as the test has the value **true**, the segment following it is evaluated followed by a new evaluation of the segment immediately following the word **repeat**. Note that the initialisation of the variables number, sum and sum.sq must take place before the word **repeat**. The reason for initialising item to 0.0 before the repeat rather than by writing

        let item := **readr**

is more subtle. Briefly, the reason is that the clause between **repeat** and **while** is syntactically separate from that following **do**. The declaration of a variable in the first clause would not be in the scope of the second clause and would lead to a syntax error being indicated.

Exercises 3

3.1 Determine the values written out by the following programs.
- (i)   **for** I = 3 **to** 7 **do write** I ?
- (ii) **for** J = 1 **to** 9 **by** 2 **do write** J ?
- (iii) **for** K = 0 **to** 15 **by** 3 **do write** K ?
- (iv) **for** L = 1 **to** 8 **by** 2 **do write** L ?
- (v)   **let** K = 3 ; **let** M = 5
      for J = K **to** M * K **by** M **rem** K **do write** J ?
- (vi) **for** I = 10 **to** 3 **by** -3 **do write** I ?

3.2 Write a program to output a heading saying 'number square cube' and then use a **for** loop to output a table of squares and cubes of integers between 1 and 20. The fifth line, for example, should read

      5   25   125

3.3 It is permissible to write a **for** clause inside a **for** clause. Work carefully through the following program step by step to see what it does.

```
for I = 1 to 5 do
begin
    write "'n",I
    let K := I * I
    for J = 1 to 3 do { write K ; K := K * I }
end ?
```

3.4 Rewrite your answer to question 3.2 using a **while** loop instead of a **for** loop.

3.5 Write a program to read in three real numbers a, b and c where a is less than b and print out a table of squares and cubes starting from a and

going in steps of c as far as you can without getting greater than b.
Thus, for example, if a = 3.10, b = 4.20 and c = 0.35 your output should
look like

number	square	cube
3.10	9.6100	29.791000
3.45	11.9025	41.063625
3.80	14.4400	54.872000
4.15	17.2225	71.473375

3.6 Write a program to read in the names of football teams together with
the number of wins, losses and draws and print out the same information
together with the total number of points giving 2 for a win, 0 for a loss
and 1 for a draw. Thus a typical line of information could be

"East Fife"   14   0   5

and the corresponding output would be

East Fife   14   0   5   33

The data should end with a team name of "****". You are not expected to
sort them into order (yet!).

3.7 Determine the values printed by each of the following program
segments

```
(i)    let i := 1
       while i < 10 do
       begin
            i := i + i
            write i,"'n"
       end

(ii)   let i := 1
       repeat
       begin
            i := i + i
            write i,"'n"
       end
       while i < 10

(iii)  let i := 1
       repeat write i,"'n"
```

                while i < 10 do i := i + i

Solutions to Exercises 3

3.1   (i)   3 4 5 6 7
       (ii) 1 3 5 7 9
      (iii) 0 3 6 9 12 15
      (iv) 1 3 5 7

Note that the output stops here because the next number will exceed 8.

      (v) 3 5 7 9 11 13 15
      (vi) 10 7 4

3.2
write "number   square   cube´n"
for I = 1 **to** 20 **do write** I,I * I,I * I * I,"´n" ?

3.3 This program writes a table of an integer, its square, cube and fourth power from 1 to 5. That is

1	1	1	1
2	4	8	16
3	9	27	81
4	16	64	256
5	25	125	625

Convince yourself by working through step by step that this is what the program does. It also works out the fifth power but does not write this out.

3.4
write "number   square   cube´n"
let I := 1   !This initialises the count
while I $\leq$ 20 **do** { **write** I,I * I,I * I * I,"´n" ; I := I + 1 } ?

3.5 This example is more difficult to do with a **for** loop since you can only count in integer steps in a **for** loop. Using a **while** loop we could write the program as follows

!J.Cole. Solution to exercise 3.5
let a := **readr** ; **let** b = **readr** ; **let** c = **readr**
while a $\leq$ b **do**
begin

```
        write a,a * a,a * a * a,"'n"
        a := a + c
end ?
```

Note that we have made a a variable but b and c are constants. It would not be wrong to make b and c variables too but it is good programming practice to declare things which are really constants like b and c by '=' rather than ':='.

3.6
```
let name := reads
while name ≠ "****" do
begin
    let wins = readi ; let losses = readi ; let draws = readi
    write name,wins,losses,draws,2 * wins + draws,"'n"
    name := reads
end ?
```

An alternative solution which only uses one **reads** command rather than two is

```
let name := ""    !This is a string with no characters in it
repeat name := reads
while name ≠ "****" do
begin
    let wins = readi ; let losses = readi ; let draws = readi
    write name,wins,losses,draws,2 * wins + draws,"'n"
end ?
```

Why do we still need the declaration of name before the **repeat** command? If you don't understand why, read the last part of Chapter 3 again.

3.7 The printed output will be

	(i)	2	(ii)	2	(iii)	1
		4		4		2
		8		8		8
		16		16		8
						16

4 IF CLAUSES

In the previous chapter we showed how sequences of clauses could be repeated a number of times. In this chapter we will look at the possibility of choosing whether a piece of program is to be executed at all, or alternatively a way in which one of two pieces of program can be chosen to be executed and the other one ignored.

In the middle of a program we often want to test some condition and if it has been met, to do something special and then carry on with the main flow of the program. For example, we might want to output a lot of numbers in the form of a table with say six numbers to a line. As we output each number we can add one to a column count and when it reaches six we can output a new line symbol. To do this we need to declare and set to zero a column count earlier in our program by a clause

    let column.count := 0

The program may be in a repetitive loop in which it is calculating new values of x say and when it outputs each new x it tests first to see how many have been output already by using the following piece of program.

```
write x
column.count := column.count + 1
if column.count = 6 do { write "'n" ; column.count := 0 }
```

Thus if the value of column.count is 6, then since we started with the value 0, six numbers have already been written out and so a new line symbol is output and the count reset to 0.

To make this quite clear let us write a whole program to print the first 42 Fibonacci numbers. The Fibonacci numbers are formed by starting with the first two both equal to 1 and always forming the next one by adding the previous two together. Thus the first few Fibonacci numbers are

            1 1 2 3 5 8 13 21 34 ....

A program to do this is as follows

```
write "Table of Fibonacci numbers'n'n"
let a := 1 ; let b := 1
write a,b                    !This prints out the two starting values
let total.no := 2            !This tells us we have printed 2 numbers
let column.count := 2        !Two columns already printed
while total.no < 42 do
begin
    let new.fib = a + b
    write new.fib
    column.count := column.count + 1
    if column.count = 6 do { write "'n" ; column.count := 0 }
    total.no := total.no + 1
    a := b ; b := new.fib   !Get ready for next Fibonacci number
end ?
```

This gives us a nice table of 7 rows and 6 columns. The numbers in a column will all be above each other since S-algol always uses 10 spaces for each integer printed unless you tell it to do something else. We will tell you how to control output yourself in a later chapter.

As in the case of the **while** clause the expression following the word **if** must be a boolean expression and will evaluate to either **true** or **false**. If it evaluates to **true** then the clause following **do** is executed. If it is **false** then the clause following **do** is skipped over.

The other type of **if** clause involves the choice of one of two alternatives. Suppose, for example, that we were reading a list of numbers successively into a variable x and we wanted to accumulate separately the sums of the negative and positive values and also the single sum of all their squares.

A piece of program to do this is

```
if x > 0 then pos.sum := pos.sum + x
         else neg.sum := neg.sum + x
sum.sq := sum.sq + x * x
```

The meaning should be obvious given that the piece of program immediately following **then** is executed if the boolean expression after **if** has the value **true** and the piece of program immediately following **else** is evaluated if this value is **false**. The final clause is executed in both cases. Note the program layout to emphasise this fact. As in Chapter 3, if we want to execute several clauses after **then** or **else** we make them into a single clause by either putting the words **begin** and **end** around them or by enclosing them in braces. We illustrate this point with a full program to carry out the above calculation but also counting the numbers in each case and printing out the averages of the three sums.

```
!J.Cole.    Averages program.
let pos.sum := 0.0 ; let num.pos := 0
let neg.sum := 0.0 ; let num.neg := 0
let sum.sq := 0.0 ; let x := readr
while x ≠ 0 do             !We suppose none of the numbers are 0
begin
    if x > 0 then { pos.sum := pos.sum + x ; num.pos := num.pos + 1 }
             else { neg.sum := neg.sum + x ; num.neg := num.neg + 1 }
    sum.sq := sum.sq + x * x
    x := readr
end
!We will assume here that neither num.pos nor num.neg is still zero
write "The mean of the positive numbers is ",pos.sum / num.pos,"´n",
      "The mean of the negative numbers is ",neg.sum / num.neg,"´n",
      "The mean of the squares is ",sum.sq / ( num.pos + num.neg ),"´n"
?
```

As in the previous example we have assumed that none of the numbers is zero and used this fact to control the **while** loop using zero to terminate the input. If we wanted to include zero as a possibility, included with the positive numbers say, we could have chosen the boolean expression after **if** to be x $\geq$ 0 and chosen some large number which could not possibly occur in the list to use in the **while** loop test. For example, if all the numbers are less than 10,000 we could have used

    while x < 10000.0 **do**

and terminated the list with 10000.0 or any greater number. We could also have used an **eof** technique.

When we first introduced the **if** .. **then** .. **else** clause we were careful to talk about the 'piece of program' following the **then** part or the **else** part. We did this deliberately because this clause can also be an expression. For example

    if a < b **then** 0.25 **else** 1.0

We could use this as part of an assignment clause as follows

cost := (**if** a < b **then** 0.25 **else** 1.0) * basic.cost

We have put the whole **if** clause in parentheses because otherwise it would be ambiguous. We would not know if ' * basic.cost ' was just multiplying the 1.0 or both the 0.25 and the 1.0. To avoid such ambiguity you should get into the habit of enclosing any such part of an expression in parentheses.

Notice there is no similar case for the **if** .. **do** because this would leave the expression unfinished if the condition were **false**. We use the word **do** because it implies that we are going to carry out some complete action such as an assignment rather than evaluating an expression which is only part of something else.

The following complete program to compute the greatest common divisor of two positive integers uses the standard mathematical technique for solving this problem.

```
let a := readi ; let b := readi
write "The g.c.d. of ",a," and ",b," is"
while a * b ≠ 0 do   !stop if either is zero
   if a > b then a := a rem b
         else b := b rem a
write if a = 0 then b else a,"'n" ?
```

Statements involving **if ... do** and **if ... then ... else** clauses are often made more complicated than necessary. For example the statement

if ch = "?" **then** query := **true else** query := **false**

can be simplified to

query := ch = "?"

We are assuming here that the variable query is of type boolean. A fuller discussion of objects of type boolean is given in Chapter 8. Similarly, the program segment

if x < 0 **then** sign := **true else**
if x > 0 **then** sign := **false else write**"Value is zero ´n"

could be simplified to

if x = 0 **then write** "Value is zero ´n" **else** sign := x < 0

To complete this chapter we write a rather silly program to teach the user a single fact. We will give a more realistic example of programmed learning when we have learned a little more about programming!

```
!J.Bloggs.  ( I am ashamed to put my name to this )
!Programmed learning. First example.
write "hello´n"
let ans := ""
while ans ≠ "China" do
begin
     write "Which country has the most people ?  "
     ans := reads
     if ans ≠ "China" do write "´nNo, the answer is China´n"
end
write "´ncorrect´n" ?
```

The above program would go on for ever if it was not given the correct answer to the question. We could modify it by putting in a count so that the program stopped after say three tries.

!J.Bloggs. Slightly better program
write "hello´n"
let ans := "" ; **let** count := 0
while ans ≠ "China" **and** count ≠ 3 **do**
begin
    write "Which country has the most people ? "
    ans := **reads** ; count := count + 1
    if ans ≠ "China" **do write** "´nNo, the answer is China´n"
end
if ans = "China"
then write "´ncorrect´n"
else write "´nHave you thought of joining a pop group as a career?´n" ?

    The boolean expression following the word **while** is more complicated than earlier examples but it still evaluates to either **true** or **false**. The boolean operator **and** tells us that the answer is **true** if both the surrounding boolean expressions are **true**. If we had used the word **or** instead of **and** then either (or both) the surrounding expressions would have to be **true** to yield the result **true**.

    At the end we tested for the answer being "China" and not for n=3 since this is what we really needed to give the required output. We know that if the answer is not "China" then n must be 3 anyway to have left the previous loop. Notice also how easy it is to modify the code to bring in new ideas and be sure that your program is still correct.

Exercises 4

4.1 Write a program to read in 3 real numbers a, b and c and check if it is possible for a triangle with sides equal in length to a, b and c to be drawn. The easiest way to do this is to calculate the semi-perimeter
        $S = (a + b + c) / 2$
and then to check if S - a, S - b and S - c are all positive. If so the triangle can be drawn. The resulting output should be readable as usual! Supply two sets of data to check that the program is working correctly.

4.2 Write a program to read in a football result such as

```
            "Colinsburgh United" 6 "St Andrews" 0
```

and to print out the same line together with one of the three comments

```
        Home Win
        Away Win
        Draw
```

4.3 Write a program to read in two words (strings) and write them out in alphabetical order. Note that if a and b are strings then a < b has the value **true** if a precedes b in a dictionary and **false** otherwise. It does not matter about the lengths of the strings being different. For this reason "dog" < "doggerel" has the value **true**.

4.4 You are captain of the starship Enterprise and you are approaching a primitive society which still measures distance in miles, yards and feet. Your range finder can read in feet to the nearest integer number of feet. Write a program to convert from feet to miles, yards and feet (1 mile = 1,760 yards, 1 yard = 3 feet) and print out the answer, leaving out a term if its value is zero. Thus your output should be able to distinguish between

```
        5287 feet = 1 mile, 2 yards, 1 foot
        5286 feet = 1 mile, 2 yards
        5281 feet = 1 mile, 1 foot
        5279 feet = 1759 yards, 2 feet
```

and so on. The tricky problem here is to leave out the commas as well!

4.5 Revision example

(i) Explain why the clause

```
        let new.fib = a + b
```

rather than

```
        let new.fib := a + b
```

is used in the Fibonacci number program. Would the last clause be wrong in this context?

(ii) Which clause in the Fibonacci program causes a possible change in the **while** clause boolean condition test ?

Solutions to Exercises 4

4.1

```
let a = readr ; let b = readr ; let c = readr
let S = 0.5 * ( a + b + c )
write "A figure with sides ",a,b,c,
     if S - a > 0 and S - b > 0 and S - c > 0 then " is "
                                              else " isn''t ",
     " a triangle'n" ?
```

You may be surprised by this solution but note that in a **write** clause list the expressions are evaluated before printing and this gives us just what we want.

Test data

        4   6   7
        3   5   9

4.2

```
!J.Cole.   Football result.
let home.team = reads ; let home.score = readi
let away.team = reads ; let away.score = readi
write home.team,home.score,away.team,away.score,"'n",
if home.score > away.score then "Home Win" else
if home.score < away.score then "Away Win" else "Draw" ?
```

4.3

```
!J.Cole. Word sort
let a = reads ; let b = reads
if a < b then write a,b
         else write b,a ?
```

4.4

```
!J.Cole. Feet to miles conversion program.
let dist = readi ; let feet = dist rem 3
let yards = ( dist div 3 ) rem 1760 ; let miles = dist div ( 3 * 1760 )
write "The distance is "
let comma := false    !This introduces a boolean variable called comma.
                      !This is the first time we have come across this
```

!idea. We will use it to test if we need to
!output a comma between terms.

if miles ≠ 0 **do**

begin

    write miles,**if** miles = 1 **then** " mile " **else** " miles "

    comma := **true**

end

if yards ≠ 0 **do**

begin

    write if comma **then** "," **else** "",yards,

    if yards = 1 **then** " yard " **else** " yards "

    comma := **true**

end

if feet ≠ 0 **do write if** comma **then** "," **else** "",feet,

                if feet = 1 **then** " foot " **else** " feet " ?

This is quite tricky but useful to be able to do. We only want to put commas between items if we have already written something. We set comma to the value **false** to start with and set it to **true** as soon as we have written something. It has to be set to **true** in both the first two **if** clauses because one or both may not be executed. When we write

        if comma ......

the boolean expression is very simple being just the boolean variable with the name comma which has the value **true** or **false**. The bad grammar that you often see in computer output is usually due either to an inflexible programming language, to bad programming or to both.

4.5

    (i) The clause is inside a sequence controlled by the **while** clause and is not given a new value inside this sequence. It would not be wrong to write := but it is better practice to indicate that objects are constant when they really are.

    (ii) The clause
        total.no := total.no + 1

5 STRINGS

We have already met string literals and we are now going to extend the idea of strings to allow us to manipulate text in our programs.

        let s = "Scotland"

declares a string constant, s, with the value "Scotland". We can join two strings together by using the concatenation operator '++'.
For example

let s1 = "Scotland" ; **let** s2 = "Ireland"
let s3 = s1 ++ " and " ++ s2
write s3 ?

will result in

        Scotland and Ireland

s3 is the result of concatenating s1, the string literal " and " and s2. String s1 is of length 8 since it has 8 characters and s2 is of length 7. " and " is of length 5 since it includes two spaces to make the final output correct. Spaces are simply characters and it is the programmer's responsibility to include these where necessary inside a string. There is a length function in S-algol which allows you to find out the length of any string. In the above program

write length(s1),length(s2),length(s3)

would give the answers

        8   7   20

As well as being able to join strings together we can also extract part of a string in order to create another. For example

        s1(5|4)

creates a new string which has the same characters as s1 starting at character 5 and copying 4 of them. Therefore

        let s4 = s1(5|4)

gives s4 the value "land".

There is one rule that may appear odd to the beginner. That is, you cannot change part of a string to something else. If you wish to change the value of a string variable you must create a new string with the correct value and assign it to the variable.
For example

let s := "Scotland"
let s1 := "Eng" ++ s(5|4)

s1 now has the value "England" and

        s1 := "Eskimo" ++ s1(4|4)

alters it to "Eskimoland". So also, of course, would "Eskimo" ++ s(5|4). In both cases the integer literals used in the substring selection can be replaced by integer expressions.

There would have been no need to introduce a new variable s1 if we had had no further need for the string literal "Scotland". It would be quite valid to write

        s := "Eng" ++ s(5|4)

This of course could only be done because s is a variable and not a constant.

We can now assign values to string variables and alter them. It is often useful to compare strings as we have already seen in previous sections. Thus in exercise 4.3 we had

let a = **reads** ; **let** b = **reads**
if a < b **then write** a,b
        else write b,a ?

This program reads in two strings and writes them out in dictionary order. Strings may have more than just alphabetic characters in them. In fact they can have any character in the ASCII code (see Appendix II). The ordering of the characters is defined by the ASCII code. However, for the present it is sufficient to know that

"a" < "z", "1" < "9", "A" < "Z", "Z" < "a" and "9" < "A"

and otherwise that the ordering is as in a dictionary.

If the two strings are not of the same length, the characters in them are compared one by one and if the strings are still equal after the comparison the shorter one is considered to be less than the longer. Thus

"Morris" < "Morrison"

One final point is that it is sometimes useful to use the empty string. This is represented by "". It has length 0 and is less than any other string in dictionary order.

To illustrate the use of strings we will now write a program to read in a string which consists of digits. The string may or may not contain leading zeros. The output from the program will be the string of digits without the leading zeros.

```
!Strip leading zeros program.
let s = reads ; let count := 1 ; let more.zeros := true
while count <= length( s ) and more.zeros do
if s( count|1 ) = "0" then count := count + 1
                     else more.zeros := false
if count > length( s ) then write "The resultant string is empty"
                       else write s( count|length( s ) - count + 1 ) ?
```

There are several things to notice about this program. The integer variable 'count' indicates the position in the string of the character that is under consideration. The boolean variable 'more.zeros' becomes **false** as soon as a non-zero leading character is found. The **while** loop terminates if 'count' gets larger than the string length or as soon as we find a character other than "0" at the beginning of the string. In this case 'count' will contain the position of the first non-zero character in the given string. The loop inspects each character in turn. Finally, we check for the situations that may occur after the loop has terminated and print out a suitable message or the required string.

You may already be getting tired of having to put quotes around strings in your data. The reason for doing this is to give the beginner as much flexibility as possible in the characters that can be used internally in strings including new line symbols. The more sophisticated user can build up his own string reading routines using the **read** command as described in Chapter 11.

In addition to the length function there are other functions associated with properties of strings. Firstly the code and decode functions are associated with the internal and external representation of characters. Characters are represented inside the computer by an ASCII code which is an integer between 0 and 127. The function code(n) takes an integer n as its argument and produces a string of length 1 representing the character n **rem** 128 as its result. Similarly, the function decode(s) takes a string s as its argument and returns the integer value of the ASCII code for the first character of s as its result.

The function letter(s) takes a string s as its argument and produces as its result a boolean value **true** if the string is of length 1 and is a letter of the alphabet, either upper or lower case and **false** otherwise. Similarly the function digit(s) takes a as its argument and produces the value **true** if that string is of length 1 and is a digit and **false** otherwise. A piece of code to test to see if a given string n is a digit and if so, to put the corresponding integer value of that digit in an integer variable i could be

    if digit(n) **do** i := decode(n) - decode("0")

For this we need to know that the ASCII codes for digits are consecutive.

Check that the right hand side of this assignment clause is correct by looking at the ASCII codes for digits.

Exercises 5

5.1 What is the length of each of the following strings?
    (i) "Ronald"

(ii)   "Jack Cole"
(iii) ""
(iv)   "'""
(v)   "Writing is done'n"

5.2 Write a program to read in a string. The string may or may not start with any number of a's or A's (or a combination of both). Write out the string without the leading a's or A's and follow this immediately with the leading part of the string that is a's or A's.

5.3 Write a program to read in the following strings

(i)   somebody's name --- name1
(ii) some social function e.g. "wedding", "birthday party" etc.
(iii) a date
(iv) a second name --- name2

and print out a letter saying
Dear <name1>,
        Thank you for your kind invitation to your <function> on <date>, which I am very pleased to accept.

                                        Yours sincerely,
                                        <name2>

where the objects in angled brackets are replaced by the data you have supplied. Do not expect the user to put in blanks around his data.

5.4 Write a program to read a string s and to find its reverse (i.e. the characters written backwards)

(i) as the value of a new string s1 leaving s unaltered
(ii) as the new value of s without using any other string variables.

Your program should still work if s is the empty string.

Solutions to Exercises 5

5.1   (i)   6
      (ii)   9
      (iii) 0
      (iv)   1
      (v)   16

Remember that '" and 'n represent one character only in a string literal.

5.2
!Program to strip leading a's or A's.
let s = reads ; let count := 1 ; let more.a.or.A := true
while count <= length(s) and more.a.or.A do
if s(count|1) = "a" or s(count|1) = "A" then count := count + 1
                else more.a.or.A := false
if s = ""
then write "This string is empty"
else write if count - 1 ≠ length(s) then s(count|length(s) - count + 1)
              else "",s(1|count - 1) ?

5.3
!Program to accept invitations.
let name1 = reads ; let function = reads
let date = reads ; let name2 = reads
write "Dear ",name1,",",'n"
for i = 1 to length(name1) + 6 do write " "
write "Thank you for your invitation to your ",function,
  "on'n ",date,", which I am very pleased to accept.'n"
for i = 1 to 30 do write " "
write "Yours sincerely,'n"
for i = 1 to 30 do write " "
write name2,"'n" ?

  If we really wanted to write a good program here we would check to see if the number of characters supplied in <function> and <date> fitted in to the line. Try modifying the program to do this assuming you do not want more than 65 characters on a line (the maximum width of a line is usually 80 for a terminal and 132 for a printer page).

5.4 (i)
let s = reads ; let s1 := ""
for i = 1 to length(s) do s1 := s(i|1) ++ s1
write "Original string is 'n",s,"'n Reversed string is 'n",s1,"'n" ?

  Work through the program to verify why it works both with empty and non-empty string.

5.4 (ii)
let s := **reads**
write "Original string is ´n",s
let len = length(s)   !Saves computing length(s) many times
for i = 1 **to** len - 1 **do**
   s := s(1|i - 1) ++ s(len|1) ++ s(i|len - i)
write "´nThe reverse string is´n",s,"´n" ?

Note the order of concatenation and also the fact that when i = 1, the second term s(1|i-1) becomes s(1|0) which is the empty string.

6 VECTORS

In many calculations we want to record linear lists or tables of objects to use in the calculation. For example, if we have been carrying out an experiment a number of times we may want to hold all the results of the experiment together and perhaps sort them into order to see which is the biggest and which is the smallest and so on. In S-algol we can use a data structure called a vector to do this. There are two basic ways in which we can declare a vector for subsequent use. There are several things, however, that we have to do in both cases. Firstly we have to say how many objects the vector is going to contain and what type these objects are. Secondly we need to be able to refer to each of the objects in the vector by some name. The usual way of doing this is to give the whole vector a name, say X, and then refer to the separate objects by using a subscript on X. Because most computer terminals do not have an easy way of printing subscripts we use the notation X(i) to mean X with subscript i. We need to know the range of the subscripts for X. That is, where they start and finish. Quite often the starting value for a subscript is 0 or 1 but it is very restrictive to insist on either of these. The simplest way to declare a vector is to write, for example

    let X = **vector** 1::8 **of** 0

This declares X to be a vector of 8 integers with subscripts going from 1 to 8 and with each integer element being set initially to 0. S-algol deduces the type of the elements in the vector from the initialising value given after the reserved word **of**. Thus if we had written

    let Y = **vector** 0::20 **of** 0.0

this would declare a vector of real numbers with 21 elements starting with subscript 0, and

        let Z = **vector** 1::100 **of** " "

would declare a vector of strings all being initialised to a single space. We point out straight away that if we subsequently give new values to the elements of Z they can be of any length. They are not restricted to their initial length or to be all of the same length.

        You may be wondering why we have used '=' and not ':='. The point is rather subtle and we will not make too much of it in this introduction. Suffice to say, there are two ways in which a vector can be made constant. Either the whole vector is a constant in the sense that we cannot assign another complete vector to that name, or else the elements of the vector are constant and cannot individually be changed. The notation '=' and ':=' are used to distinguish between constant and variable complete vectors. Do not worry about this too much if you do not really understand it - you really need to know some more about programming and to read the later chapters of this book. If you stick to using '=' in declaring vectors for most of the examples in this book you will not get into difficulties. We also discuss the point further a little later on in this chapter.

        Having declared a vector we can assign values to individual elements by clauses like

        X(i) := 3

where i is a previously declared integer with a value between 1 and 8 (look back at the declaration of X). S-algol checks for you that the value of the subscript i is indeed in the correct range and that the value being assigned to the element is of the correct type.

        Suppose that we wanted to read in 10 real numbers and print out the smallest and the biggest. We could do this without using a vector but we will use one to illustrate the ideas.

```
let x = vector 1::10 of 0.0
for i = 1 to 10 do x( i ) := readr
let smallest := x( 1 ) ; let largest := x( 1 )
!The above line starts things off with x( 1 ) for both values
for i = 2 to 10 do
```

```
begin
    if x( i ) < smallest do smallest := x( i )
    if x( i ) > largest do largest := x( i )
end
write "The smallest number is ",smallest,
    " and the largest is ",largest ?
```

We will now write a more ambitious program to read in a list of real numbers and sort them into order. We will do this by writing one for loop inside another one with the inner loop range getting smaller and smaller. At each stage in the inner loop we will put the smallest object to the bottom of the part of the vector under consideration.

```
let n = readi         !This gives the number of objects
let x = vector 1::n of 0.0
for i = 1 to n do x( i ) := readr
!sort code starts here
for i = 1 to n - 1 do
begin
    let smallest := x( i ) ; let k := i
    for j = i + 1 to n do
        if x( j ) < smallest do { smallest := x( j ) ; k := j }
    if k ≠ i do { x( k ) := x( i ) ; x( i ) := smallest }
end
write "The sorted list of ",n," numbers is'n'n"
for i = 1 to n do write x( i ),"'n" ?
```

You should try working through this program step by step with say n = 5 doing exactly what S-algol does.

If you start off with the numbers 1.3 6.6 1.1 2.8 3.7 the order at the end of each loop will be

1.1	6.6	1.3	2.8	3.7
1.1	1.3	6.6	2.8	3.7
1.1	1.3	2.8	6.6	3.7
1.1	1.3	2.8	3.7	6.6

Notice that we have declared the vector x with subscripts

going from 1 to n. Under the appropriate circumstances either of the limits of a vector can be written more generally as any integer expression.

Quite often we want to use two-dimensional vectors, that is tables with both rows and columns. We can declare such a vector by writing a list of subscript limits as follows.

      let p = **vector** 1::10,1::8 **of** 0

We like to look at this as a vector of vectors rather than as a two-dimensional array for a reason we will explain shortly. In this case it is a vector with 10 elements, each element of which is a vector of integers with 8 elements.

There are two ways in which we can refer to particular elements in such a vector of vectors. The usual shorthand method is to write p(i,j) to represent the i,jth element but it is also permissible to write p(i)(j). This form is clumsier and will not usually be used when referring to individual elements. We note however that p(i) does have a meaning, namely the whole vector in the ith position in p. This is quite a sophisticated but powerful idea whose use we will illustrate shortly.

Let us consider first an example to read in a table of real numbers with n rows and m columns and to form a new vector containing the row sums. We can do this easily as follows

```
let p = vector 1::n,1::m of 0.0
for i = 1 to n do
   for j = 1 to m do p( i,j ) := readr      !Reads in values by rows
let p.rowsum = vector 1::n of 0.0
for i = 1 to n do
   for j = 1 to m do p.rowsum( i ) := p.rowsum( i ) + p( i,j )
```

A slightly more elegant program would be

```
let p = vector 1::n,1::m of 0.0
let p.rowsums = vector 1::n of 0.0
for i = 1 to n do
   for j = 1 to m do
   begin
        p( i,j ) := readr
```

```
        p.rowsums( i ) := p.rowsums( i ) + p( i,j )
   end
```

A common problem is to sort the rows of a table of values into order depending on the values in some particular column. Suppose we want to do this with the above vector of vectors p and for the rth column where 1 < r < m. We can do this with a simple modification to the sort loop of the program given above.

```
let n = readi ; let m = readi
let p = vector 1::n 1::m of 0.0
for i = 1 to n do
   for j = 1 to m do p( i,j ) := readr
let r = readi                          !column for sort key
for i = 1 to m - 1 do
begin
    let smallest := p( i ) ; let k := i
    for j = i + 1 to m do
       if p( j,r ) < smallest( r ) do { smallest := p( j ) ; k := j }
    if k ≠ i do { p( k ) := p( i ) ; p( i ) := smallest }
end
```

Note that smallest is the name of a vector which is initially the ith row of p. The comparison of elements

$$p(j,r) < smallest(r)$$

has correct subscripts since p is a vector of vectors and smallest is a vector. Finally, whenever a change of row is required, this is done by changing the row pointers rather than the individual elements. Note however that it is not possible to change columns in this way. One should therefore think carefully about choosing the order in which vectors of vectors are defined.

In each of the above examples we have initialised the vector elements all to the same value. Although we have used 0 for integers we can use any integer expression for initialisation and similarly for vectors with elements of other types. Quite often we want to initialise vector elements to a collection of different values. We could do this by reading data into them, but if we always need the same values for a particular program it would be better to do it as part of the program. In S-algol we do it by a clause of the following sort.

      let t = @1 **of int**[1,2,3,4,5,6]

This needs some explanation. The notation @1 is an indication of where the subscripting is to start. This we call the lower bound. The value 1 can be replaced by any integer expression. The words **of int** say that the elements in the vector are all to be of type integer and furthermore are variables. If we want them to be constants we would write **of cint** instead. The actual values are given as an expression list enclosed in square brackets. We do not need to give the upper bound of the vector since S-algol will count the elements for us.

If we want to initialise a vector of reals like

      let X = @0 **of real**[0.0,1.0,-3.7,2.0]

we do not need to put in the decimal point in the integers since S-algol will convert them for us as we have seen earlier. We could thus write

      let X = @0 **of real**[0,1,-3.7,2]

As another example we will write

let days = @1 **of cstring**["Sun","Mon","Tues","Wed","Thurs","Fri","Sat"]

Note that the strings need not all be of the same length.

The flexibility of the vector notation allows the data structures to be of any complexity that we wish. We could for example write

let triangular.array = @1 **of *cint**[@1 **of cint**[1],
                                          @1 **of cint**[1,1],
                                          @1 **of cint**[1,2,1],
                                          @1 **of cint**[1,3,3,1],
                                          @1 **of cint**[1,4,6,4,1]]

to give a representation of the Pascal triangle

     1
     1   1
     1   2   1
     1   3   3   1

            1   4   6   4   1

The type ***cint** used above indicates that each object in the vector 'triangular.array' is itself a vector of objects of type **cint**. We discuss this further below.

To illustrate these ideas we will give an example which, given the day of the week on which a given month starts and a date within the month, will work out which day of the week it falls on. We have to think of a way of solving the problem before we can program it. First of all we must find if the day given for the start of the month is the 1st, 2nd......7th day of the week. Call this i. Then we find the remainder on division by 7 of the actual day given. Call this date. If date = 0 then the actual day is the same as i, if date = 1 then the day is i + 1 and so on. The actual day requested is therefore always

            (date + i) **rem** 7

A program to do this is

!Program to find the day of the week.
let days = @0 **of cstring**["Sunday","Monday","Tuesday","Wednesday",
                      "Thursday","Friday","Saturday"]
let first.day = **reads**
let i := 0
while first.day ≠ days(i) **do** i := i + 1
let date = **readi**
write "Day ",date," of the month falls on a ",days((i + date) **rem** 7) ?

In introducing the concept of a vector we have not mentioned the data type of this sort of object. The elements of a vector can be of type integer, real, boolean, string or indeed vector or any other data type in the language. The data type of a vector is denoted by an '*'. Thus a vector with integer elements is of type ***int** if the elements are variable and ***cint** if the elements are constant. A vector declared by using ':=' is itself variable and may have other vectors assigned to it whereas if it is declared by '=' it is constant.

Thus if we had written

let X := @1 **of int**[1,2,3]
let Y := @1 **of int**[6,7,8,9]

we can write later on in our program

        X := Y

and X will now have the same value as Y i.e the same vector. Note that in this case, the elements of the original X are now lost for ever.

    If we had used

        let X = @1 **of int**[1,2,3]

then the subsequent

        X := Y

would be invalid since X is a constant.

    Since vectors may be assigned, it is often necessary to interrogate the vector to find its bounds. The functions **upb** and **lwb** are provided in S-algol for this purpose. Thus if q is a vector defined by

        let q = @1 **of int**[2,4,6,8,10,12]

then **upb**(q) has value 6 and **lwb**(q) has value 1.

    Similarly, if s is a vector of vectors defined by

        let s = **vector** 0::6,1::10 **of** ""

then **upb**(s) has value 6, **lwb**(s) has value 0 but **upb**(s(3)) has value 10 and **lwb**(s(3)) has value 1.

    There is no reason why vectors of vectors of vectors and so on should not be defined. S-algol allows you to do this by an obvious extension to the notation. Thus, for example, one can define

        let t = **vector** 1::8,1::6,1::3 **of** 0

and so on.

Exercises 6

6.1 Why in the example to sort numbers have we declared vector x with an '=' but use ':=' to assign a value to x(i)?

6.2 A bubble sort works in the following way. Given a vector of size n, the first scan of the bubble sort works from 1 to n - 1 looking at successive pairs of numbers. If the first is less than or equal to the second they are left unaltered. Otherwise they are swapped. At the end of this scan the largest will be at the top. Repeat the process with n-1 elements, excluding the top one which is in the correct place, until all the elements are sorted. Write a program to do this.

Warning. If you need to swap the elements of a vector it is not correct to write

x(i) := x(j) ; x(j) := x(i)

because the first assignment destroys the old value of x(i). You will need to write

let temp = x(i) ; x(i) := x(j) ; x(j) := temp

6.3 Bubble sort can be stopped as soon as you do not have to change anything in one complete scan. Modify your program above to set a boolean variable to **false** if any change is made in the order and test it to see if you need to continue. You will need to use a **while** clause rather than a **for** clause for this program.

Note that bubblesort is one of the most inefficient methods of sorting.

6.4 Write a program to output all the verses of "On the twelfth day of Christmas". If you can do this without looking at the solution you are well on the way to becoming a programmer! (Unless you just write out the song word for word).

6.5 Write a program to read in a list of words, each one as a string, and sort them into dictionary order.

6.6 Suppose x is a vector of vectors defined as

let x = @1 **of** *****cint**[@1 **of** **int**[1,1],
@4 **of** **int**[1,2,1],
@1 **of** **int**[1,2,3,2,1],
@1 **of** **int**[1,2,1],
@-2 **of** **int**[1,1]]

Determine the value of **upb** and **lwb** for each of the following

x   x(2)   x(3)   x(5)

Solutions to Exercises 6

6.1 The '=' sign implies that the vector as a complete object cannot be assigned to. Its individual elements can be assigned to and this is why we can use ´:=´.

6.2
!J.Cole. Bubble sort program.
let n = **readi**
let x = **vector** 1::n **of** 0.0
for i = 1 **to** n **do** x(i) := **readr**
!bubble sort starts here
for i = 1 **to** n - 1 **do**
   for j = 1 **to** n - i **do**
   if x(j) > x(j + 1) **do**
   begin
       let temp = x(j)
       x(j) := x(j + 1)
       x(j + 1) := temp
   end
!now write out the answers
write "The sorted numbers are´n´n"
for i = 1 **to** n **do write** x(i),"´n" ?

If you did not succeed in solving this yourself try working through the solution step by step with a vector of say 4 elements.

6.3 We change the piece of program between the two comments as follows

!bubble sort starts here
let i := 1 ; **let** more := **true**
while i ≤ n **and** more **do**
begin
    more := **false**
    for j = 1 **to** n - i **do**
    begin
        if x(j) > x(j + 1) **do**
        begin
           let temp = x(j)
           x(j) := x(j + 1)
           x(j + 1) := temp
           more := **true**

```
              end
        end
        i := i + 1
end
!now write out the answers


6.4
!the first day of Christmas, five verses only. Extra verses need only
!a change of data.
let phrase1 = "'nOn the"
let phrase2 = " day of Christmas'nmy true love sent to me'n"
let number = @1 of cstring[ " first"," second"," third"," fourth"," fifth" ]
let gift = @1 of cstring[
           " a partridge in a pear tree'n",
           " two turtle doves'n",
           " three french hens'n",
           " four calling birds'n",
           " five gold rings'n" ]
!calculation starts here
write " The five days of Christmas'n'n"
!The first verse is a special case because the word 'and' is not used.
write phrase1,number( 1 ),phrase2,gift( 1 )
!remainder of verse production starts here
let next.verse := " and" ++ gift( 1 )
for i = 2 to 5 do
begin
     next.verse := gift( i ) ++ next.verse
     write phrase1,number( i ),phrase2,next.verse
end ?
```

6.5 The solution is exactly the same as either of the two sort examples given earlier but you need to change the clauses including **readr** to **reads** and also the vector declaration to a vector of strings.

6.6   upb(x) = 5   lwb(x) = 1
                upb(x(2)) = 6   lwb(x(2)) = 4
                upb(x(3)) = 5   lwb(x(3)) = 1
                upb(x(5)) = -1   lwb(x(5)) = -2

7 THE CASE CLAUSE

Programs are often complicated to read because of the amount of testing and branching inside them. The **if** ... **then** .... **else** clause is a very useful one but even this can be unreadable when similar clauses are nested in the two different parts of the clause itself. The **case** clause in S-algol is a very powerful one and we introduce it as usual with an example.

```
case party of
"lab"    : no.lab  := no.lab  + 1
"cons"   : no.cons := no.cons + 1
"lib"    : no.lib  := no.lib  + 1
"snp"    : no.snp  := no.snp  + 1
"comm"   : no.comm := no.comm + 1
default  : no.rest := no.rest + 1
```

We are assuming here that 'party' is the name of a string which is used to hold the political affiliation of a person and the effect is to add one to the corresponding total of members of that party. In the general case the name 'party' can be replaced by any expression of any type and the string literals before the colons can be replaced by expressions of that same type or even lists of expressions of that type separated by commas. The effect is that the expression following the word **case** is evaluated and its value is then compared one by one with the values of the expressions, or members of the list of expressions, preceding the colon. As soon as a match is found further comparison stops and the clause (or, when relevant, the expression) following the colon is executed. The program then skips over the rest of the **case** clause to the next part of the program. Thus, whereas the **if** clause allows the selection

of one of two alternatives to be executed, the **case** clause allows one of
many. If no match is found then the **default** option is obeyed
automatically. A **default** option must always be written. This is good
programming practice to make sure that you have not overlooked a case but
in the rare case in which you do not need it you should include either

default : { }

or

default : { **write** "No case matches.Value ## returned´n" ; ## }
!Note that ## must be replaced by a value of the correct type
!e.g. 0 or "" etc.

An example of a case when all the options are expressions is

```
no.of.legs := case animal of
                 "cat","dog","horse","cow"  : 4
                 "man"                      : 2
                 "ant"                      : 6
                 "triffid"                  : 3
                 default                    : 0
```

Some programming languages have a variant on the **case** clause
which branches depending on the value of an integer expression only.
Usually the programming has been contorted to obtain the appropriate
integer before the **case** clause is executed but in our case we do not
usually need to think of this. In the rare case in which we do need to use
a test for integer values we can write

case integer **of**
1 : ...
2 : ...
9 : ...
default : ...

There is no significance in this example finishing with 9. There is no
restriction on the number of choices.

In the rest of this chapter we give a number of examples of
the use and power of the S-algol **case** clause.

A common example in introductory books on programming is the solution of a quadratic equation. If a proper solution is given it is often quite complicated but the following should be immediately understandable. We use here the square root function sqrt which is supported automatically by S-algol.

```
write "Input three real coefficients "
let a = readr ; let b = readr ; let c = readr
if a = 0.0 then write "This is not a quadratic since a = 0´n" else
begin
    let discrim = b * b - 4.0 * a * c ; let den = 2.0 * a
    case true of
    discrim < -1e-6 : write "Imaginary Roots are ",-b / den,
                            " + or - i * ",sqrt( -discrim )/den,"´n"
    discrim > 1e-6  : begin
                        let r1 = ( -b + sqrt( discrim ) )/den
                        write "Real Roots are ",r1,
                              " and ",c/( a * r1 ),"´n"
                      end
    default         : write "Single Root is ",-b/den,"´n"
end ?
```

The apparent complication of the discrim > 1e-6 case is nothing to do with the programming but with the computation to produce an accurate result in all cases. If you do not believe this try solving the equation

$$0.08 \, x^2 + 21.4 \, x + 0.14 = 0$$

and substituting the answers back in the left hand side to see how near to 0 you get. If you just calculate -b $\pm$ sqrt(b * b - 4 * a * c) you will get bad results for one root. The use of **true** as the expression following **case** is a particularly useful one. We test each of the following conditions to find the first one which is also **true** for our particular equation.

In the next example we are going to write a program which will read in a French regular verb, find its root and ending and print out the first person singular conjugation of the verb. Our program is not intelligent enough to find out if the verb given is not a regular verb unless its ending is wrong. So if, for example you give it "etre" it will work out the present tense as if it were regular.

```
write "Type a French regular verb "
let verb = reads
let pronoun = case verb( 1|1 ) of
              "a","e","h","i","o","u" : "j´´"
              default             : "je "
let ending = case verb( length( verb ) - 1|2 ) of
             "er"    : "e"
             "ir"    : "is"
             "re"    : "s"
             default : "x"
if ending = "x" then write verb," is not a French regular verb´n"
                else write "The first person present tense of ",verb,
                           " is ",pronoun,verb( 1|length( verb ) - 2 ),
                           ending,"´n" ?
```

Note that the setting of 'pronoun' is determined by testing for a vowel and the **default** is for the remaining consonants.

Suppose now that we have the results of a survey on a pop record with the survey information being for each participant.

    age   sex   opinion

where age is an integer, sex is "m" or "f" and opinion is "yes" or "no". Suppose we have a lot of such data terminated by a single entry of age = 0 and we wish to find the following totals.

    (i)   number of females < 20 who like the record
   (ii)   number of females $\geq$ 20 who like the record
  (iii)   number of females < 20 who dislike the record
   (iv)   number of females $\geq$ 20 who dislike the record
    (v)   number of males < 20 who like the record
   (vi)   number of males $\geq$ 20 who like the record
  (vii)   number of males < 20 who dislike the record
 (viii)   number of males $\geq$ 20 who dislike the record

We will write the part of the program which accumulates the totals and leave the writing out of the results to you.

```
let sums = vector 1::8 of 0
let age := readi
while age ≠ 0 do
begin
     let sex = reads ; let opinion = reads
     let index =
     case true of
     sex = "f" and age <  20 and opinion = "yes" : 1
     sex = "f" and age ≥  20 and opinion = "yes" : 2
     sex = "f" and age <  20 and opinion = "no"  : 3
     sex = "f" and age ≥  20 and opinion = "no"  : 4
     sex = "m" and age <  20 and opinion = "yes" : 5
     sex = "m" and age ≥  20 and opinion = "yes" : 6
     sex = "m" and age <  20 and opinion = "no"  : 7
     sex = "m" and age ≥  20 and opinion = "no"  : 8
     default : { write "Invalid data ",age,sex,opinion,
                       "'nType corrected data 'n" ; 0 }
     if index ≠ 0 do sums( index ) := sums( index ) + 1
     age := readi
end
```

Note how the **default** option picks up invalid data. Although this program is readable it is still not a good program because it has a great deal of almost repetitive writing in it. You could simplify the program by writing instead of the **case** clause

```
let I = ( if sex = "f" then 1 else 5 ) +
        ( if age < 20 then 0 else 1 ) +
        ( if opinion = "yes" then 0 else 2 )
sums( I ) := sums( I ) + 1
```

but it is not nearly so obvious what you are doing and if you make a mistake it is more difficult to pick up. Furthermore, you still have to check each data line for possible errors. A better, and still readable solution is to replace the **case** clause by the following piece of program.

```
let i = case sex of
        "f"        : case opinion of
                        "yes"    : if age < 20 then 1 else 2
                        "no"     : if age ≥ 20 then 3 else 4
                        default : 0
        "m"        : case opinion of
                        "yes"    : if age < 20 then 5 else 6
                        "no"     : if age ≥ 20 then 7 else 8
                        default : 0
        default : 0
if i = 0 then write "Error in data ",age,sex,opinion,"´n"
         else sums( i ) := sums( i ) + 1
```

We have again used a value of i = 0 to detect errors in the string responses. We could have been more explicit using 0 for an error in opinion and -1 for an error in sex say.

Exercises 7

7.1 Write a program which will read in three real numbers and check whether a triangle with sides of these lengths exists and if so whether it is scalene, isosceles or equilateral. Think carefully before you start writing your program to decide the tests you need to find the result. If you cannot do this look at the hint at the bottom of these exercises before the solutions and then write the program.

7.2 Write a **case** clause which sets a name ´colour´ to a colour shown for the following objects.

```
         "grass"           "green"
         "fire engine"     "red"
         "leaf"            "green"
         "daffodil"        "yellow"
         "carrot"          "orange"
         "pillar box"      "red"
         "emerald"         "green"
         anything else     "black"
```

7.3 Write a program to calculate sums for different combinations for any particular survey data you like to choose. (For example, a survey of school dinners!)

Hint for solution of 7.1. If you test in a **case** clause in the following order, each test is simple.
        1. test if it is a triangle.
        2. test if it is equilateral. That is a = b **and** b = c.
        3. test if it is scalene. That is a ≠ b **and** b ≠ c **and** c ≠ a.
        4. **default** it must be isosceles.

Solutions to Exercises 7

7.1
!J.Cole. Test triangles.
write "Input three real numbers as sides of a triangle "
let a = **readr** ; **let** b = **readr** ; **let** c = **readr**
let s = 0.5 * (a + b + c)
write "The figure with sides ´n",a,b,c,
      case true of
      s < a **or** s < b **or** s < c   : " is not a triangle´n"
      a = b **and** b = c   : " is an equilateral triangle´n"
      a ≠ b **and** b ≠ c **and** c ≠ a   : " is a scalene triangle´n"
      default   : " is an isosceles triangle´n" ?

7.2
colour := **case** object **of**
        "grass","leaf","emerald"   : "green"
        "fire engine","pillar box" : "red"
        "daffodil"   : "yellow"
        "carrot"   : "orange"
        default   : "black"

7.3 This depends on your choice of survey data but the program will be very similar to the example about a pop record in the above chapter but with different expressions in the **case** clause.

8 SOME IMPORTANT ODDS AND ENDS

We now clear up some points we left unfinished in the preceding chapters and also introduce a few new ideas. Since there are a lot of different topics covered we will use section headings in this chapter.

8.1 Write facilities

We will discuss briefly the way in which you can control your output rather more precisely than hitherto. We have already introduced the special character 'n as part of a string literal. 'n is the new line symbol. There are four other special symbols of this type.

'o allows overprinting of the current line. That is, it causes the printing to go back to the start of the line you have just completed. The use of this is to enable underlining to be done easily or to overprint characters if you are building up pictures.

'b causes the printer to backspace one place. This gives the same facility as 'o but for just one character. Clearly you can backspace as many characters as you like in a loop.

't is for typewriters or terminals with a tabulate facility. If you do not know what this means forget it!

'p makes the printer skip to a new page.

Note that some of these will give strange results when used on videos where overprinting does not work correctly.

We have assumed that our output for integers and reals is always of the same size. As a default option S-algol gives you 10 places for an integer and 12 for each real plus two extra spaces after each number printed. There are three ways in which you can control this part of the output.

1. You can reset the default options by setting any of a number of system predefined variables to new values. These variables are

> (a) i.w which controls the integer width. Thus i.w := 6 would set integer width output to 6 until you change it again. i.w is already known to the system, as are the others in this section, and you do not have to redeclare it with a **let** clause.
> (b) r.w is the same as i.w except that it is for the width of reals.
> (c) s.w sets the spaces left after printing integers or reals. The default value is 2.

2. You can specify the output size for any particular expression by writing ':' followed by an integer expression in a **write** clause. Thus

> **write** i : 6,0.5 * x : 10,j : n,"z" : 8

would give 6 spaces for i, 10 spaces for 0.5 * x, n spaces for j where n is some integer calculated in your program and 7 spaces followed by a z. All output is right justified, which explains why "z" : 8 is output as 7 spaces followed by z. You may not realise the full power of this at the moment but it is a very powerful output control facility. If, using either of the above methods, a number will not fit into the space allocated then it is expanded to fit into the smallest possible space.

3. There are two system functions called eformat and fformat which give you another means of controlling output of real numbers. We do not want to go into detail here for beginners but for the more experienced programmers we will say that eformat and fformat take three parameters which are the real number and the number of places before and after the decimal point respectively. Thus in a **write** clause you could include

> **write** fformat(x,3,2)

to give the value of x an output format with 3 places before the decimal point, the decimal point itself and 2 places after it. If the numbers cannot be printed correctly in the form you have specified S-algol will ignore the specification and print them in the usual manner.

8.2 Operator priorities

Standard arithmetic notation is ambiguous. It is not obvious whether the value of

3 + 2 * 5

is 13 or 25. We are taught at school that multiplication has priority over addition so the 'correct' answer is 13 but this is only a convention. We will however keep to this convention ourselves and note that multiplication and division have equal highest priority and addition and subtraction have lower but also equal priority. If ambiguity still remains then we work from left to right. Thus

6 - 4 - 1

has value 1. Note that **div** and **rem** have equal priority to / and *.

The boolean negation ~ has the next highest priority followed by the relational operators for comparing two objects, namely

= ≠ < > ≤ ≥

all of which have equal priority followed by the boolean connectives **and** and **or** both on their own. The complete order of priorities is

/ * div rem ++
+ -
~
= ≠ < > ≤ ≥
and
or
|

8.3 Simple data types

We have introduced four simple data types so far. These are integer, real, string and boolean and when we spoke about initialising vectors we introduced the corresponding reserved words **int**, **cint**, **real**, **creal**, **string** and **cstring** for variable and constant integer, real and string elements respectively. We have used the boolean literals **true** and **false** and there are two corresponding reserved words to indicate the type boolean, namely **bool** and **cbool**. This apparently curious choice is traditional in computing. **bool** is an abbreviation for boolean which is derived from the name of George Boole, a mathematician, who developed a branch of mathematics which became known as boolean algebra. For example, we use **bool** and **cbool** to declare boolean vectors as follows

       let B = @1 **of bool**[true,true,false,false]

or

       let BB = @-3 **of cbool**[x **or** y,x **and** y,~y]

We can also write

       let D = **vector** 1::8 **of true**

or

       let E = **vector** 0::6 **of false**

An example of the use of a vector of booleans is given later in Chapter 12.

8.4 Abort

The reserved word **abort** simply stops the program.

8.5 Functions

We have already mentioned the length and sqrt functions. They are used by giving the name of an object or an expression in brackets after the function name. Thus

       sqrt(5 + 4)

has the value 3.0 and

       length("abc" ++ "def")

has the value 6.

There are a number of other functions which are commonly used and they are listed in Appendix IV. Do not worry about the formality of the declarations. You will understand them after reading the chapter on procedures. As an example if you want to use sin(x) and cos(x) in your program you can write for example

       y := a * cos(x) ; b * sin(x)

Note that the argument is enclosed in brackets. The comment after each definition in Appendix IV tells you the type for the argument where appropriate.

8.6 Standard Identifiers

A number of standard identifiers exist in the language. They are

r.w	variable initially 12
s.w	variable initially 2
i.w	variable initially 10
s.i	variable set to the standard input
s.o	variable set to the standard output
maxint	constant, the maximum integer
epsilon	constant, the largest real e such that $1 + e = 1$
pi	constant, pi
maxreal	constant, the largest real

Note that the minimum integer value is -maxint - 1 and the minimum real value is -maxreal.

8.7 Semi-Colons

As a lexical rule in S-algol, a semi-colon may be omitted whenever it is used as a separator and it coincides with a newline. This, of course, allows many of the annoying semi-colons in a program to be left out.

However, to help the compiler deduce where the semi-colons should be, it is a rule that a line may not begin with an binary operator.

e.g.
```
        a *
        b       is valid
```
but
```
        a
        * b       is not
```

This rule also applies to the invisible operator between a vector and its index list.

e.g.
```
        let b = a( 1,2 )       is valid
```
but
```
        let b = a
               ( 1,2 )
```

will be misinterpreted since vectors can be assigned

8.8 Comments

Comments may be placed in a program by using the symbol '!'. Anything between the ! and the end of the line is regarded by the compiler as a comment.

e.g.   a + b   ! add a and b

8.9 Directives

There are certain compiler directives used to annotate the listing of the program provided by the compiler that the user may wish to invoke. The symbol '%' is used to denote a directive. They are

%list   print the program listing.
%nolist   do not print the program listing.
%title,< string literal >   take a new page and use the string as a heading
                            for this and subsequent pages.
%lines,< integer literal > Inform the compiler of the number of lines
                            on each page of output paper.
%ul   underline the reserved words in the listing.
%noul   turn off the reserved word underlining.

Exercises 8

8.1 In chapter 3 we wrote a program to print a shopping list. Rewrite the output part so that you do not have to worry about keeping the name of the article strings to the same length when preparing the data.

8.2 Determine the value of the following expressions. To compare your answers to the solution, put in appropriate brackets first to show how the priorities operate.

(i)   3 * 2 + 4 * 8 - 6 * 2
(ii) 8 **div** 4 **div** 2
(iii) 3.0 + 6.1 / 2.0 + 1.3
(iv) **true and ~false or false**

8.3 We have seen how we can print a given string in a field of a given width using : n. This right justifies the string inserting the number of blanks required to the left. Thus if 'name' is less than 20 characters long

            name : 20

in a write list, right justifies the name in a field of length 20. Write output list elements to write 'name' left justified in a field of length 20.

8.4 Modify the program in section 5.3 to put your address at the top right hand side of your page which is 75 characters wide. Again do not expect the user to put in leading blanks. You should expect them to supply something like

>"20, Castle Drive,"
>>"St Andrews,"
>>>"Fife"

Solutions to Exercises 8

8.1   **write** quantity,name : 14," at ",cost.per.item,line.total,"'n"

8.2   (i)   ((3 * 2) + (4 * 8)) - (6 * 2) = 26
     (ii)   ((8 **div** 4) **div** 2) = 1
     (iii)   ((3.0 + (6.1 / 2.0)) + 1.3) = 7.35
     (iv)   ((**true and** (~**false**)) **or false**)
               = ((**true and true**) **or false**)
                = **true or true**
                = **true**

8.3   name,"" : 20 - length(name)
We need two write list entries here. 'name' is printed as itself followed by 20 - length(name) blanks.

8.4
!Program to accept invitations.
let name1 = **reads** ; **let** function = **reads**
let date = **reads** ; **let** name2 = **reads**
while ~eof **do**
begin
     let address = **reads**
     write address : 55 + length(address) +
               (20 - length(address)) **div** 2
end
write "Dear ",name1,",'n"
write "" : length(name1) + 6

write "Thank you for your invitation to your ",function,
      "on´n ",date,", which I am very pleased to accept.´n"
write "Yours sincerely,´n" : 47
write name2 : 30 + length(name2) ?

Note that 55 + length(address) + (20 - length(address)) **div** 2
simplifies to   65 + length(address) **div** 2

9 PROCEDURES

The programs we are now writing are more complicated than before because the actual problems themselves are also becoming more complicated. One of the aims of a good programming language is to keep the programs readable so that a lot of program documentation is unnecessary. To help us keep programs more readable we introduce the idea of a procedure. The idea is that we can write a section of program and give a name to it and then 'call' this piece of program or procedure from somewhere else in the main program, or indeed from another procedure.

This idea leads us to think about writing programs in a different way. Instead of trying to carry everything in our heads and then write the program as a long linear list of instructions we start off by thinking of the solution in general terms and then gradually refine the general solution to a complete solution of the problem. Such a method is called a top down solution. We illustrate this idea with a few simple examples.

In example 6.2 we wrote a bubble sort program. In the middle of this we wrote a piece of code

```
if x( j ) > x( j + 1 ) do
begin
     let temp = x( j )
     x( j ) := x( j + 1 )
     x( j + 1 ) : = temp
end
```

which swapped the values of x(j) and x(j + 1) if x(j) > x(j + 1). This particular piece of program is not very difficult to read but we will write a procedure to make it even clearer. When we were writing our program we could have written

        if x(j) > x(j + 1) **do** swap.xs

and finished writing our program, delaying writing the detailed code for the swap operation until later. We could then have written a procedure with name swap.xs as follows.

procedure swap.xs
{ **let** temp = x(j) ; x(j) := x(j + 1) ; x(j + 1) := temp }

        The sequence of clauses, or procedure body as it is correctly called in this case, is exactly the same as in the previous program but the advantage is that the main program is more immediately understandable and we delayed thinking about how to write the code until later. The effect of the procedure call swap.xs in the **if** clause is simply to transfer control to the body of the procedure and when this has finished executing to return control back to the main program.

        The name swap.xs was chosen to make it clear to the reader what has to be done in the procedure body. The rule for inventing such names is the same as for any other name in S-algol, namely it must start with a letter and be made up of letters, digits and dots only. We will shortly see how to pass information to the procedure body. In the above case the information has come from the main program itself and the declarations of the objects used in the procedure body apart from 'temp' have already been made in the main program. 'temp' is purely a local name.

        There are two other points to remember about writing procedures. First of all, although we actually wrote our procedure after the main program we still have to insert it in the program before we make the call itself. This is because the S-algol compiler is a fast one which does all its compilation in a single scan. In order to set up the program links between the call and the procedure it needs to know about the procedure before the call is made. It can come anywhere in your program before the call but after the declaration of the main body objects that it uses. S-algol recognises the word **procedure** in the heading of the procedure declaration and knows that it does not have to execute any code at that moment.

        The other point which we have briefly mentioned in the last paragraph, is that in order to compile the code into machine instructions

S-algol needs to know about the names which have an existence outside the procedure. In the swap.xs procedure there were names x and j which were used. This implies a knowledge of x and j. We would therefore have to put our procedure swap.xs declaration immediately after the piece of code

for j = i + 1 **to** n **do**
begin

This is not very nice, could be very confusing and may easily lead to errors which would prevent your program compiling if you were to put this declaration in the wrong place. If we stop to think a little more carefully about the procedure we can see that it is a special case of a more general procedure to swap 2 vector elements, say z(i) and z(j) or on another occasion t(m) and t(n). This leads us to the idea of a procedure with parameters. We use the notation

procedure swap(***real** T ; **cint** i,k)
{ **let** temp = T(i) ; T(i) := T(k) ; T(k) := temp }

In the brackets after the procedure name swap we have declared the use of a vector T and two integer constants i and k. We call these the formal parameters of the procedure. The word 'parameters' just means that they are names special to the procedure and they are called formal because they are just used to show how the computation has to be carried out in the procedure body. The notation ***real** is used to indicate that T is a vector of reals. In our main program we still call the procedure by writing its name but we now have to say what the actual parameters are. In our case the call would be in

if x(j) > x(j + 1) **do** swap(x,j,j + 1)

The effect of this call is to execute the code as defined in the procedure declaration but with the formal parameters T, i and k given the values of x, j and j + 1 respectively. Note that the constant 'temp' is local to the procedure and has no existence outside the procedure body. The procedure is now independent of the actual parameters until it is called and so its declaration can be placed anywhere we like in the program so long as it precedes the call.

If somewhere else in our program we wanted to swap two other actual real vector elements, say p(s) and p(t) we could write

    swap(p,s,t)

and the same procedure would swap their values.

One further point about the use of ***real** T. We declare our formal parameter as a vector in this way because we do not want to tie ourselves down to a fixed length of vector. Although we have introduced the idea of formal parameters which are declared along with their type in the procedure heading this does not prevent us from using parameterless procedures, like our first definition of swap.xs, if it is convenient to do so.

Suppose now, instead of just writing a program to read in n numbers and sort them into order we wanted to sort some numbers as part of a much larger program. It would be convenient to write a procedure called sort say, to do this. Such a procedure could then be used in several different programs and would also help in making the main program more readable.

We need to think first about the parameters that we require. The numbers we wish to sort will always be in a vector so the vector name will be one parameter. We sometimes want only part of the vector so it would be useful to give the sort limits as two integers i and j say. Since we will need this procedure later on we will make the vector of type **int** and in a similar manner to the above we do this by using the formal parameter

    *int q

meaning a vector of integers called q. (If we wanted a vector of vectors we would write ****int** q and so on.) Our full declaration of the procedure could now be

```
procedure swap( *int x ; int i,j )
{ let temp = x( i ) ; x( i ) := x( j ) ; x( j ) := temp }
procedure sort( *int q ; int i,j )
begin
    for s = i to j - 1 do
    for t = s + 1 to j do if q( s ) > q( t ) do swap( q,s,t )
```

end

Note that the declaration of procedure swap must precede the declaration of procedure sort since sort uses swap internally. An actual call of the procedure sort could be

    sort(x,1,n)

which would sort the vector of integers called x from x(1) to x(n) into order. In the main program we would have declared an integer vector x with subscripts including the range 1 to n.

So long as it makes sense we can use expressions in place of simple object names in the actual parameter list. In the above example it does not make sense to replace the actual vector parameter by an expression. It does, however, make sense to replace i and j by expressions. We could for example write

    sort(y,i,i + 10)

and this would sort the eleven integers from y(i) to y(i + 10) into order.

The two procedures we have used above both consisted of complete pieces of code which could have been written in a sequence directly in the main program. We chose not to do this largely to make our programs more readable but also to save repeating code if we made more than one call of the procedure in the program.

Sometimes we would like to evaluate an expression and return its value as the result of a procedure call. For example we may have to evaluate a number of quadratic expressions in a program and it would be convenient to write a procedure to do this for us. We need to be clear about the type of answer we are going to produce and in S-algol we need to declare this along with the formal parameters. For example the quadratic producing procedure could be

procedure quadratic(**real** a,b,c,x -> **real**)
a * x * x + b * x + c

Here we have simply written the expression we want to evaluate as the procedure body and have indicated in the procedure heading by ->

real that the result is going to be real.

From the computational point of view it would have been slightly better to have written the actual calculation as

(a * x + b) * x + c

This happens to save one multiplication operation but is also more accurate in awkward cases where for example x is nearly equal to zero. It also suggests a way in which we can write a procedure to evaluate a polynomial for an arbitrary value of n. The following procedure will do this for us with 'a' being a vector of coefficients of the polynomial.

procedure polynomial(***real** a ; **real** x ; **int** n -> **real**)
begin
    let p := a(n)
    for i = n - 1 **to** 0 **by** -1 **do** p := p * x + a(i)
    p
end

This is a slightly more complicated example in which we have to execute a sequence before producing the answer. When we have to do this, we need to make it clear just what the required answer is and this accounts for 'p' being on the last line before the word **end**. If it is necessary, 'p' can be replaced by an expression which evaluates to the required answer. Thus our quadratic example is really a special case of this when there is no extra calculation to be done before computing the answer. Before you read on you should convince yourself that this procedure does calculate a polynomial as required. Try taking n = 3 and work through the **for** clause step by step.

To conclude this chapter we give a few more simple examples of procedure declarations and calls.

In chapter 4 we wrote a program to compute Fibonacci numbers and included a piece of the main program to write these out, six to a line. We will write a procedure to do the output but will make it more flexible for more general use. We have to think carefully first of all about the parameters and the global names that we need. The piece of code that we are going to convert to a procedure is

```
write new.fib
column.count := column.count +1
if column.count = 6 do { write "'n" ; column.count := 0 }
```

To make this more general we will replace the literal 6 by a name say no.in.line and make this a parameter of the procedure. It would also be more flexible if we could control the integer output width as described in chapter 8 so we will include a second integer parameter called width to do this. The integer variable column.count presents a difficulty. The value that it holds is not local to the procedure since it needs to be passed in from the main program and the updated value remembered by the main program for the next time that the procedure is called. This leads us to think rather carefully about the properties of the parameters of the procedure. In S-algol we say that all parameters are 'called by value'. This means that the values of the parameters at call time are passed into the procedure body and any assignments to the formal parameters inside the procedure body are purely local to the procedure. That is, the values of the corresponding actual parameters in the main program are not altered by such assignments. Declarations of parameters are thus equivalent to the declarations of local names with initial values assigned by the procedure call. Methods of handling parameters are the subject of much discussion by language designers and we do not wish to elaborate on our choice here. We will simply say that we believe that this method of parameter passing leads to fewer program run time errors, than **apparently** more flexible systems do. We can easily overcome the problem of the global value of column.count by declaring it in our main program before we declare the procedure. It thus becomes available for use in the subsequent procedures since the procedure declaration is in the scope of the name. We can rewrite the program as follows

```
write "Table of Fibonacci numbers'n'n"
let a := 1 ; let b := 1 ; let field.width = 10
write a:field.width,b:field.width
let total.no := 2 ; let column.count := 2
procedure output.no( int number,no.in.line,width )
begin
```

```
        write number : width
        column.count := column.count + 1
        if column.count = no.in.line do
        begin
              write "'n"
              column.count := 0
        end
end
while total.no < 42 do
begin
      let new.fib = a + b
      output.no( new.fib,6,field.width )
      a := b ; b := new.fib
      total.no := total.no + 1
end ?
```

We often want to leave several blank lines before output lines and it is useful to have a procedure to do this for us. The first example we give is for the case when we want the procedure to issue its own **write** command. Such a procedure could be

```
procedure lines( int n )
for i = 1 to n do write "'n"
```

A subsequent call lines(3) will output three new lines in the output stream.
We may also want a procedure to output a string of new line symbols 'n to include as part of a **write** clause list in the main program or another procedure. Such a procedure could be

```
procedure new.lines( int n -> string )
begin
      let s := ""
      for i = 1 to n do s := s ++ "'n"
      s
end
```

and it could be used in a **write** clause as, for example

write "Title of output",newlines(3)
for i = 1 **to** m **do write** a(i),b(i),c(i),new.lines(1)

to produce a title followed by two blank lines and then the table of values, 3 on a line for m lines.

The observant reader may have noticed that despite our statement that parameters are called by value and that if we change the value of a parameter inside a procedure, its global value is unaltered, nevertheless in the procedure the actual values of the elements of the vector have been changed to sort them into the correct order. This is a difficult point to make clear and one which **appears** to be an exception to the rule. Formally, if x is a vector parameter of a procedure, we can assign a new vector to x inside the procedure without changing its value externally. In the sorting example we are not changing the whole vector but rather elements of the vector.

Another useful idea which is common to most algol-like languages is that of recursive and mutually recursive procedures. In Chapter 11 we will discuss the way in which recursive procedures can be used to obtain elegant and readable solutions to some difficult problems but here we will just introduce the ideas with a simple example.

Suppose that we want to read an integer n typed by a user as data for a program and to refuse to accept it until a value between 1 and 10 say is typed. With the knowledge we have so far we could write a piece of program

```
let not.done := true
write "Enter an integer between 1 and 10 "
while not.done do
begin
    n := readi
    if n < 1 or n > 10
    then write "Integer must be between 1 and 10. Try again"
    else not.done := false
end
```

Another solution would be to write a procedure called get.integer as follows:

procedure get.integer(-> **int**)
begin
    let n = **readi**
    if n < 1 **or** n > 10 **then**
    begin
        write "The integer must be between 1 and 10. Try again"
        get.integer
    end else n
end

Note that both branches of the **if ... then ... else ...** clause produce an integer answer which is the result produced by the procedure.

The procedure could now be used in the main program by writing

write "Enter an integer between 1 and 10"
n := get.integer

You might try generalising this example by adding two integer parameters lower.bound and upper.bound to the procedure definition so that the same procedure can be used from different parts of the program with different integer bounds on the data. Don't forget to change the message to take account of this.

The idea of mutual recursion involves two or more procedures which call each other. It is difficult to give meaningful elementary examples of this idea but perhaps the following will suffice.

Suppose we wish to program a computer game in which there are two types of move called move.a and move.b but in the code for move.a it is possible to call move.b and vice versa. For the sake of the illustration suppose both move.a and move.b use board co-ordinates x,y and a status indicator called status. Then the procedures could be

procedure move.a(**int** x,y,status)
begin
   . . . . . .
   if status = 1 **do** move.b(p,q,1)
   . . . . . .

end
procedure move.b(**int** x,y,status)
begin

. . . . . .

   if status > 3 **do** move.a(j,k,status)

. . . . . .

end

A technical problem with this piece of code is that the procedure move.a calls move.b before it has been declared and vice versa if we change the order of the two procedures.

We overcome this problem by insisting that for mutually recursive procedures, the existence of a procedure yet to be declared must be notified by a **forward** declaration before the first procedure in which it is to be used. For the above example we would do this by putting the **forward** declaration

forward move.b(**int,int,int**)

immediately before the procedure declaration for move.a.

This **forward** declaration tells the compiler that the declaration of procedure move.b with three integer parameters, which are not named at this point, is to follow later. In order to avoid some rather nasty computational ambiguities which we will not go into here it is necessary to insist that if a **forward** declaration is used, only other procedure declarations and structure class declarations (see Chapter 10) can be written between the **forward** declaration and the corresponding actual procedure declaration itself.

Exercises 9

9.1 Write a procedure without parameters to calculate the distance between two points (x1,x2), (y1,y2). Remember that the square of the distance is

$$(x1 - y1)^2 + (x2 - y2)^2$$

9.2 Modify the procedure in 9.1 to be a procedure with parameters x1,y1,x2,y2.

9.3 Use the procedure in 9.2 to write a program to find the pair of points in a list of points (x(i),y(i)) (i = 1,2, ... n) whose distance from each other is maximum for the list.

9.4 Write a procedure which given two integers as actual parameters returns the value of the larger as the result.

9.5 Write a procedure which given a string as a parameter returns the value **true** if the first character is a vowel and **false** otherwise.

9.6 Write a procedure to

  (i) discard any leading spaces or new line characters in the input stream.

  (ii) accumulate the string of characters from this point until the next new line character and return this string as its result.

  You may use the function **peek** which allows you to look ahead to the next character without actually reading it.

  Note that this procedure can be used to read a response from a terminal as a string without enclosing that string in quotation marks.

Solutions to Exercises 9

9.1
procedure dist(-> **real**)
sqrt((x1 - x2) * (x1 - x2) + (y1 - y2) * (y1 - y2))

9.2
procedure dist(**real** x1,x2,y1,y2 -> **real**)
sqrt((x1 - x2) * (x1 - x2) + (y1 - y2) * (y1 - y2))

9.3
let n = **readi**
let x = **vector** 1::n **of** 0.0
let y = **vector** 1::n **of** 0.0
for i = 1 **to** n **do** { x(i) := **readr** ; y(i) := **readr** }
!The vectors x and y are now initialised
!Let i,j be the subscripts of the required points
!initially we set both to 1 and distance to 0.0
!Note that we can work with the distance squared and take
!the square root at the end.
let i := 1 ; **let** j := 1 ; **let** dist := 0.0
!We write a procedure dsq to work out the

!square of the distance between the
!two points (a,b), (c,d)
!It is unnecessary to find the square root at this point.
procedure dsq(**real** a,b,c,d -> **real**)
(a - c) * (a - c) + (b - d) * (b - d)
for p = 1 **to** n - 1 **do**
for q = p + 1 **to** n **do**
begin
    let d = dsq(x(p),y(p),x(q),y(q))
    if d > dist **do** { dist := d ; i := p ; j := q }
end
write "The greatest distance is between points ",i," and ",j,
    "´nwith values ",x(i),y(i),x(j),y(j),
    " and the distance equals ",sqrt(dist) ?

9.4
procedure bigger(**int** i,j -> **int**)
if i ≥ j **then** i **else** j

9.5
procedure vowel(**string** s -> **bool**)
s ≠ "" **and** (**case** s(1|1) **of**
        "a","e","i","o","u" : true
        default   : false)

9.6
procedure read.the.line(-> **string**)
begin
    let s := ""
    repeat s := **read while** s = " " **or** s = "´n"
    while peek ≠ "´n" **do** s := s ++ **read**
    s
end

        The function **read** allows you to read the next character in the input stream without the character being enclosed in string quotes.

10 STRUCTURES

It is often useful to collect together several pieces of information and give a name to this collection. We are not referring here to a vector which we have already discussed but rather to something like information about a person. We may wish to read information about a person's name, home town, age and sex say and hold this as one unit of data. We can do this by declaring a structure as follows

structure person(**string** name,home.town ; **int** age ; **string** sex)

This defines the form of the structure and gives names to the items which make up the structure and also a name, that is 'person', to this type of structure. We can now set up an **instance** of such a structure by, for example

    let joe := person(**reads,reads,readi,reads**)

This sets up a structure of the given type and allows us to refer to joe's name by writing joe(name) and so on. As usual, the read commands can be replaced by any relevant expressions that you wish. To set up a complete file of people, say members of class A4 in a given school, we could use a vector of structures as follows.

structure person(**string** name,home.town ; **int** age ; **string** sex)
let no.in.class = **readi**
let A4 = **vector** 1::no.in.class **of nil**
!The above clauses set up a vector of pointers. (see next paragraph)
for i = 1 **to** no.in.class **do** A4(i) := person(**reads,reads,readi,reads**)
!We could now write a program to sort them into any order.

We now have a vector with elements containing this

information. Although in this example each structure is of the same class, it is not necessary. The piece of program above includes the declaration of a vector of **nil**. This is a vector of pointers, or more correctly of type ***pntr** in S-algol. The pointers are used to point at structures. Initially they are set to **nil** which is a predefined name of type **pntr** in S-algol, and later in the **for** loop they are made to point at different instances of 'person'.

If we wanted now to work out the average age of the class we could do it as follows.

let total.age := 0
for i = 1 **to** no.in.class **do** total.age := total.age + A4(i)(age)
let average.age = total.age / no.in.class

As with vectors an alternative notation to

A4(i)(age)

is

A4(i,age)

which is probably more readable but that is a matter of opinion.

We can also use **pntr**s in, for example, a new structure definition. Suppose we wished to set up a parental family tree structure. We could do this by defining a structure

structure child(**string** name ; **pntr** father,mother)

and we could set these pointers to the appropriate people when we read in the data. If we want to make this structure into a real family tree going both ways then we need to handle pointers to children as well. We can do this by ensuring that the children entry in the structure is of a variable length. That is, a vector of pointers to children. We use the notation

*pntr children

to denote a vector of pointers with the name children. The complete definition could then be

structure human(**string** name ; **pntr** father,mother ; ***pntr** children)

If we want to refer to the ith child of a vector of human structures with the name 'Jack' we would write

Jack(children)(i) or Jack(children,i)

In the following example we are going to help Albert the domino player to play a hand of seven dominoes. Albert plays according to very strict rules. Whenever he has to play he chooses the domino by the following rules.

(a) look at the total number of spots on the domino and play the one with the highest total

(b) if rule (a) fails, Albert always prefers to play a double e.g 2/2 is played before 3/1

(c) finally if rule (b) fails, Albert will then play the domino with the biggest single field e.g. 1/5 is played before 2/4

First of all we have to decide how to represent the information we need for the calculation. Each domino has two fields and because of rule (c) we require to know the larger. Also rule (a) will require the sum of the two fields. Therefore the domino can be represented by the structure

structure domino(**cint** larger,smaller,sum)

We make the fields constant integers since once we have created them they will never be altered. There are seven dominoes in a hand and we can represent this by a vector of pointers to structures, each element eventually pointing at a domino structure. Initially we declare the vector of pointers by

let dom = **vector** 1::7 **of nil**

We will now write the program to put the hand into order

input.dominoes
sort.dominoes
output.hand
?

The main program consists of three procedure calls which will now be refined until we have a complete program. Let us write the procedure input.dominoes

procedure input.dominoes
for i = 1 **to** 7 **do**
begin
    let x = **readi** ; **let** y = **readi**
    dom(i) := **if** x < y **then** domino(y,x,x + y)
                  else domino(x,y,x + y)
end

Seven pairs of integers are read in and the seven vector elements are made to point at structures representing each domino.

We are now going to sort the vector so that the first element will contain the best domino to be played and so on. Notice that the values in the structures are not being altered, only the vector elements which point to them. For the sorting we can use bubblesort

procedure sort.dominoes
for i = 1 **to** 6 **do**
for j = i + 1 **to** 7 **do**
if ~greater(dom(i),dom(j)) **do** swap(dom,i,j)

This is essentially the same solution as exercise 6.2. However we have abstracted the solution for clarity and we must now write procedures 'swap' and 'greater'. 'swap' can be written by

procedure swap(***pntr** t ; **int** i,j)
{ **let** temp = t(i) ; t(i) := t(j) ; t(j) := temp }

which is familiar. Procedure 'greater' decides which is the more desirable of the two dominoes according to the rules. The result of this procedure is either **true** or **false** and is therefore boolean.

procedure greater(**pntr** t,t1 -> **bool**)
t(sum) > t1(sum) **or**

t(sum) = tl(sum) **and**
(t(larger) = t(smaller) **or**
 tl(larger) ≠ tl(smaller) **and**
 t(larger) > tl(larger))

You should satisfy yourself that this largish boolean expression represents the 3 rules for playing dominoes. All we have to do now is to output the hand.

procedure output.hand
begin
    write "Albert's hand in preferred order is :- "
    for i = 1 **to** 7 **do**
    write dom(i,larger)," | ",dom(i,smaller),"'n"
end

Careful attention should be paid to the method of solution to this problem. First, the data structures to represent the information required were decided upon. Procedures were then used successively to refine the solution until a program was obtained and finally we put it all together to give the required result. The procedures must be put in the proper order so that none is referred to before it is declared. This gives us the full program.

structure domino(**cint** larger,smaller,sum)
let dom = **vector** 1::7 **of nil**
procedure input.dominoes
for i = 1 **to** 7 **do**
begin
    let x = readi ; **let** y = readi
    dom(i) := **if** x < y **then** domino(y,x,x + y)
                        else domino(x,y,x + y)
end
procedure greater(**pntr** t,tl -> **bool**)
t(sum) > tl(sum) **or**
t(sum) = tl(sum) **and**
(t(larger) = t(smaller) **or**

```
        t1( larger ) ≠ t1( smaller ) and
        t( larger ) > t1( larger ) )
procedure swap( *pntr t ; int i,j )
{ let temp = t( i ) ; t( i ) := t( j ) ; t( j ) := temp }
procedure sort.dominoes
for i = 1 to 6 do
for j = i + 1 to 7 do
if ~greater( dom( i ),dom( j ) ) do swap( dom,i,j )
procedure output.hand
begin
     write "Albert's hand in preferred order is :- "
     for i = 1 to 7 do
     write dom( i,larger )," | ",dom( i,smaller ),"'n"
end
!Main Program
input.dominoes
sort.dominoes
output.hand
 ?
```

A **pntr** may point to a structure of any class. In the same way that it is useful to interrogate a vector to find its bounds it is also useful to test a pointer for the class of the structure it is currently pointing at. Two relational operators **is** and **isnt** are provided for this purpose. For example if we have

```
        structure golfer( cint no.of.rounds,no.of.clubs )
        structure cricketer( cstring name ; cint no.of.runs )
```

and

```
        let first = golfer( 4,14 )
        let second = cricketer( "Peter",1192 )
```

then

```
        first is golfer      yields the value true
```

and

```
        second isnt cricketer yields the value false
```

The full power of **is** and **isnt** is realised when writing general purpose procedures to process a large number of structure classes.

Sorting

Structures can also be used for sorting. So far we have only used bubblesort or variations of it in our programs. Bubblesort is however very inefficient. If there are n elements to be sorted then the number of sorting operations is proportional to n^2. We can do much better than this.

We have already seen how a family tree can be modelled using structures. That is one kind of tree. Another special kind of tree which is useful in sorting is a binary tree. Each node in a binary tree has a left and a right subtree which may be empty. When used for sorting the tree is ordered such that for any node the elements on the left subtree are all less than the elements of the current node and the elements on the right are greater or equal. The following is a sorted binary tree

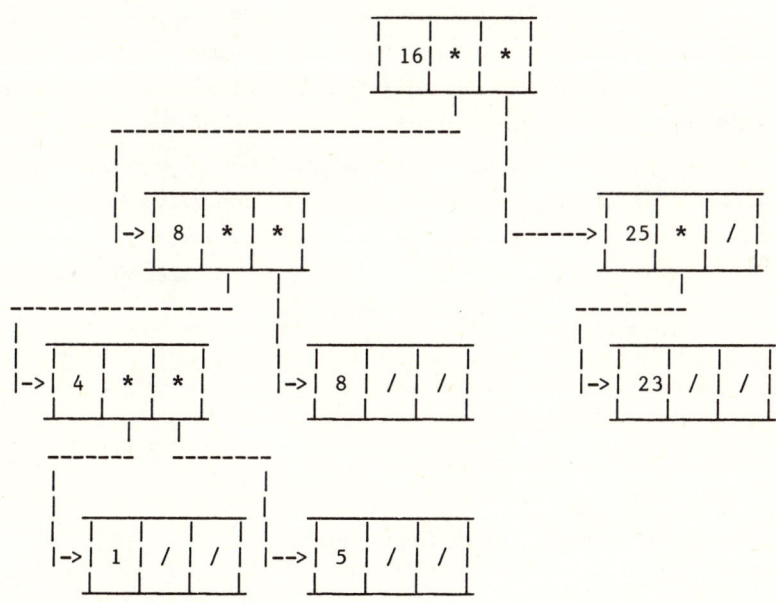

The fields with an '*' in them contain pointers to the **next** structure. Those with '/' all point to **nil**. The top of the tree is called the head or the root. In constructing an ordered binary tree the

head initially points to **nil**. We will now write a program to read in strings and sort them as they are read, using a binary tree for the sorting.

The structure to hold the data is

structure tree.node(**cstring** tree.string ; **pntr** left,right)

This defines the structure to hold a string and a left and right subtree which will be used for the nodes of the tree. The main program is

```
let head := nil
while ~eof do head := enter( head,tree.node( reads,nil,nil ) )
write "The sorted strings are :-´n"
print.tree
?
```

This initialises the head of the tree to **nil** and then goes round a loop adding entries to the tree using procedure enter. The enter procedure which we still have to write, takes as parameters the head of the tree and the new node and returns the new head of the tree.

If the tree is empty then the new head of the tree is the new node. If the tree is not empty then the new string value is compared with the string in the head node. If the new node is less than the head node we place the new node on the left subtree and otherwise on the right subtree. The following code will do this.

```
procedure enter( cpntr head,new -> pntr )
if head = nil then new else
if new( tree.string ) < head( tree.string ) then
begin
      head( left ) := enter( head( left ),new )
      head
end else
begin
      head( right ) := enter( head( right ),new )
      head
end
```

The subtlety of the solution is that it uses recursion to take advantage of the recursive nature of the tree definition. At any node, the left and right subtree are either empty or not. The procedure enter may therefore be used to add new nodes to these subtrees.

Having set up the ordered tree we now have to extract the values in the correct order. To do this we perform a left to right scan of the tree. This is called a **symmetric order** traversal of the tree. That is, at any node in the tree we print the values in the left hand subtree then the current value followed by the values in the right hand subtree. This is again recursive.

```
procedure print.tree( cpntr head )
if head ≠ nil do
begin
     print.tree( head( left ) )
     write head( tree.string ),"'n"
     print.tree( head( right ) )
end
```

For those in the know, this procedure is the same as the solution to the Towers of Hanoi problem (see Chapter 12) except that it uses data structures. The reader should satisfy himself that the program is complete.

The advantage of this type of sorting is that it is fast. For n elements the number of sorting operations is roughly proportional to nlog(n) which is much less that n^2 for large values of n.

Exercises 10

10.1 A linked list is a list of structures that are linked together through one of their fields. For example, a linked list of integers may be constructed out of the structure

```
structure int.list( int number ; pntr link )
```

by the program segment

```
let list := nil
```

```
for i = 1 to 3 do list := int.list( i,list )
```

This will result in the list

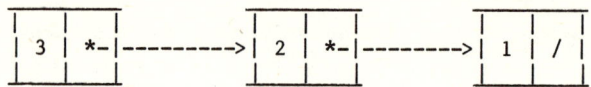

pointed at by list.

Given an integer and a list write procedures to perform the following

    (i)   add a structure containing the integer to the start of the list.

    (ii) add a structure containing the integer to the end of the list.

    (iii) assuming the list is ordered from high to low, add a structure containing the integer in such a way as to preserve the ordering.

10.2 Write a procedure to reverse a list of the above type.

10.3 Define a structure to hold information about oil wells. The structure fields should include the name of the well, its map reference, the number of men on the well, output per day in barrels and nearest neighbouring oil well.

Solutions to Exercises 10

10.1

(i)
```
procedure add.start( int i ; pntr list -> pntr )
int.list( i,list )
```

(ii)
```
procedure add.end( int i ; pntr list -> pntr )
if list = nil then int.list( i,nil ) else
begin
     let temp := list
     while temp( link ) ≠ nil do temp := temp( link )
     temp( link ) := int.list( i,nil )
```

```
            list
end

(iii)
procedure add.order( int i ; pntr list -> pntr )
if list = nil or list( number ) ≤ i then int.list( i,list ) else
begin
      let temp := list
      while temp( link ) ≠ nil and temp( link,number ) > i
            do temp := temp( link )
      temp( link ) := int.list( i,temp( link ) )
      list
end
```

10.2
```
procedure reverse.list( pntr list -> pntr )
begin
      let temp := nil
      while list ≠ nil do
      begin
            temp := int.list( list( number ),temp )
            list := list( link )
      end
      temp
end
```

10.3
```
structure oil.well( string well.name
                    int ref.east,ref.north,no.men,barrels
                    pntr nearest.well )
```

11 ADVANCED INPUT AND OUTPUT

So far we have said very little about files. This is because we did not wish to confuse the issue of S-algol as a programming language with the particular environment in which S-algol resides. For S-algol to be an effective programming tool it must provide the ability to communicate with the outside world to receive data and produce results. The outside world in this case is the operating system of the host computer. The three main implementations of S-algol are for the operating systems **VAX/VMS**, **UNIX** and **CP/M**.

So that the S-algol programmer can take advantage of the power of the host operating system, the S-algol language reflects the operating system's facilities. The one drawback of this is that the operating systems are very different from one another. Thus the implementations of S-algol differ in some respects. It is good programming practice to isolate the sections of your program that are dependent on the operating system's facilities as this will make it easier to transport your programs from system to system. Indeed the S-algol compiler itself is written in this manner making good use of the separate compilation facilities of the language (see later).

S-algol communicates with the outside world via files. To create an object of type **file** we must 'open' or 'create' the file in the file system. This will be a different action depending on the operating system involved. The following discussion is based on the VAX/VMS implementation of S-algol but if you are using a different operating system you should consult the definitions of the following functions.

The first two S-algol functions allow the user to create a new file or open an existing one. The functions are defined by

procedure create(**string** name,org,F.type,R.type

               int R.length -> **file**)

procedure open(**string** name,F.type ; **int** access.mode -> **file**)

These functions take a number of parameters that are as yet unexplained and produce an object of type **file** which we call a **file descriptor**. The file descriptor can now be used anywhere an object of type **file** is legal and in particular in **read** and **output** clauses. For example

           let input.file = open("Ronsfile","a",0)

would allow us to write clauses like

           let c = **readi**(input.file)

in which case the integer will be read from the file called 'Ronsfile' instead of the standard input (i.e. the user's terminal). The interpretation of the parameters in the create and open functions are as follows.

file.name   a valid VMS file name.
     org   an 's' denotes a sequential file,and an 'r' denotes a relative file (VMS terminology).
  F.type   files may be binary (consisting of 8 bit bytes) or ASCII (consisting of 7 bit ASCII characters). If a file is an ASCII file, then the line feed character is expanded on output to carriage return, line feed and similarly carriage return, line feed is collapsed into a line feed on input. An 'a' denotes an ASCII file, a 'b' a binary file. Note : the terminal is an ASCII file.
  R.type   'f' for fixed length records, 'v' for variable length records.
R.length   maximum length in bytes or characters of a record.
access.mode   0 for read only, 1 for write only, 2 for reading and writing.

If an attempt to open or create a file fails, the **file** literal value of **nullfile** is returned. This value may be used as follows.

let s = "a.bad.file"
let the.file = open(s,"a",0)   !try to open a read only ASCII file
if the.file = **nullfile do** ! was the open a success

```
begin
    write "The file ",s," cannot be opened'n"
    abort
end
```

Once you have finished with a file it should be closed. 'close' closes a file and allows no further access to it during the program unless it is re-opened. All files with write permission, which have been opened or created within the program, should be explicitly closed by use of this procedure. The procedure is defined by

> **procedure** close(**cfile** descriptor)

and in the above example we could write

> close(input.file)

to close the file.

The 'seek' operation is only allowed on relative files. It allows access to a particular record of a file, that is it aligns the file such that the next **read**, or **write** will take place at the start of the selected record. The procedure is defined by

> **procedure** seek(**cfile** file.desc; **cint** multiple,key)

with the parameter 'key' interpreted as follows:
- 0   add 'multiple' to the current record number and align the file at the resulting record.
- 1   use 'multiple' as an absolute record number. Hence if 'multiple' = 0, the file is aligned at the start of the first record.
- 2   or any other integer add 'multiple' to the number of the last record in the file and align at the start of the resulting record. In this case 'multiple' is usually zero or negative.

Finally the 'flush' standard procedure takes a file descriptor as argument and flushes the buffer associated with it. The function is defined by

> **procedure** flush(**cfile** f)

This function is only used when we wish to ensure that a particular write operation has taken place. Normally input and output to files is buffered in store for efficiency. The flush operation ensures that the buffer has indeed been written out. There is usually no need to use the flush operation as the system will perform it automatically when necessary.

Every S-algol program has two rather special files defined for it called the standard input ´s.i´ and the standard output ´s.o´. These names are predefined for you and are variables of type **file**. The standard input and output files are usually the computer terminal but they may be reassigned to other files if required. The files are special in that they are taken as the default in **read** and **write** clauses. e.g.

>   **let** s = **reads**

is shorthand for

>   **let** s = **reads**(s.i)

and the same is true for all the other read clauses as well as **eof**.

Normally a file acts as a continuous stream of ASCII characters. The action of reading from a file has the effect of forming the characters at the current position in the file into a literal of the type of object specified in the **read** clause and moving the current position in the file on to the character following the literal just read. If the literal cannot be formed correctly then an error message will be issued. Also when reading reals or integers certain punctuation that precedes the literal will be elided in the file. Punctuation consists of newlines, spaces and tabs. A summary of all the input clauses is given below

read	read the next character in the file.
readi	ignore preceding punctuation and read an integer literal.
readr	ignore punctuation and read a real literal.
readb	ignore punctuation and read a boolean literal.
reads	ignore punctuation and read a string literal.
peek	look at the next character without reading it.
read.a.line	read from the current position up to a newline symbol. Give the result as a string without the newline symbol.

read.byte read one 8 bit byte as an integer.
   eof test for end of file.

Of these functions **read, reads, peek** and **read.a.line** are of type **string, readi** and **read.byte** of type **int, readr** of type **real** and **readb** and **eof** of type **bool**. When we wish to read from another file we simply change ´s.i´ to another file descriptor by assigning to it or by replacing it in the read clause. For example

   let total = **readi**(input.file)

will read an integer from the file with descriptor ´input.file´ and use it to initialise the constant ´total´.

One function that we have not seen before is **read.byte**. As was mentioned earlier all the input and output to files is performed using ASCII characters. Not all I/O devices operate using the ASCII character set which is a seven bit code. Furthermore it is often useful to read binary information. Thus S-algol provides a function that will read a byte (8 bits) of information from a file and give the result as an integer between 0 and 255. An example of the use of such a function could be to read two bytes from a file and form them into an integer. The following procedure will do this.

procedure form.integer(cfile F -> **int**)
b.or(shift.l(**read.byte**(F),8),**read.byte**(F))

Output to files is slightly different. The clause

   write "hello´n"

is a short form of

   output s.o,"hello´n"

Like **write**, **output** may also take a list of items to be written out. When we wish to write to another file we simply change ´s.o´ to a new file descriptor in the **output** clause.

We should also mention that there is a reciprocal function to **read.byte** called **out.byte**. The clause

   out.byte out,163,0

takes the zeroth (least significant) byte of the integer 163 and writes all 8 bits to the file 'out'.

Exercises 11

11.1 Write a program to open a VMS ASCII file and read all the text writing out only the first 15 characters of each line.

11.2 Write a program that will copy a VMS ASCII file changing all lower case letters to upper case.

11.3 Write a procedure that will read an S-algol name. Since a name must start with a letter the procedure should take that letter as an input parameter. The procedure then reads letters, digits and dots to form the name. Take care not to read more characters than is necessary.

11.4 Write a program to read a VMS binary file and append the contents to an existing VMS ASCII relative file converting from binary to ASCII as you go.

Solutions to Exercises 11

11.1
```
let F = "Input"
let input = open( F,"a",0 )
if input = nullfile then write "Cannot open file ",F,"'n" else
begin
      while ~eof( input ) do
      begin
            let s = read.a.line( input )
            if length( s ) ≥ 15 then write s( 1|15 )
                                 else write s
            write "'n"
      end
      close( input )
end
 ?
```

11.2
```
let F = "Input" ; let F1 = "Output"
let in = open( F,"a",0 )
```

```
if in = nullfile then write "Cannot open file ",F,"´n" else
begin
      let out = create( F1,"s","a","v",256 )
      if out = nullfile then write "Cannot create file ",F1,"´n" else
      begin
            let case.diff = decode( "a" ) - decode( "A" )
            while ~eof( in ) do
            begin
                  let s := read( in )
                  output out,if s >= "a" and s <= "z"
                               then code( decode( s ) - case.diff )
                               else s
            end
            close( out )
      end
      close( in )
end
 ?

11.3
procedure read.an.identifier( cstring s -> string )
begin
      let result := s ; let s1 := peek
      while letter( s1 ) or digit( s1 ) or s1 = "." do
      begin
            result := result ++ read
            s1 := peek
      end
      result
end

11.4
procedure error( cstring s,s1 )
write "´nCannot ",s," file ",s1,"´n"
let F = "Input" ; let F1 = "Output"
let in = open( F,"b",0 )
if in = nullfile then error( "open",F ) else
begin
```

```
        let out = open( F1,"a",2 )
        if out = nullfile then error( "open",F1 ) else
        begin
              seek( out,1,2 )
              while ~eof( in ) do output out,code( read.byte( in ) )
              close( out )
        end
        close( in )
end ?
```

Note the parameterised error function and the use of the code function which is defined in Chapter 8.

12 SOME COMPLETE PROGRAMMING EXAMPLES

In this chapter we will discuss some complete programming examples starting with a discussion of the problem to be solved, the broad principles of the computer solution and finally the development of the program.

Consider the problem of producing a table of primes up to some given integer n. The method used will be that of the traditional Sieve of Eratosthenes which notionally sets up a vector of all the integers between 1 and n and then deletes all the composite numbers which are multiples of 2, 3, 5 and so on, leaving only the primes. At each stage in the process we find the next prime by scanning through the vector from the last prime found looking for the next undeleted entry. It is only necessary to carry out the process up to the largest integer not greater than the square root of n since any number between this and n cannot possibly be exactly divided by any number greater than or equal to root n without the dividend being less than root n itself.

The obvious solution of setting up a vector of integers from 1 to n can be improved upon when we reflect that it is never necessary to inspect the values stored in the vector. We always know that the initial value in the ith element is i. The solution is simplified by declaring a boolean vector p of values **true** and setting them to **false** as composite numbers are 'scored out'. We also note that when we consider a prime i, we do not want to erase i itself but only composite numbers with factor i. The first such number will be 2 * i followed by every ith element from that point. The basic loop for eliminating multiples of i from a given prime i onwards is therefore

for j = 2 * i **to** n **by** i **do** p(j) := **false**

The fact that composite numbers may be set to **false** several times does not matter.

We need only enclose this in a loop which counts from 2 to the integer part of the square root of n and to execute the inner loop whenever p(i) corresponds to a prime, that is, has value **true**. The required double loop is

```
for i = 2 to truncate( sqrt( n ) ) do
if p( i ) do
for j = 2 * i to n by i do p( j ) := false
```

You should convince yourself that this piece of program works correctly by tracing its execution through with a small value of n, say n = 15.

The rest of the program simply reads in the value of n, declares the vector p and writes out the results neatly. This leads us to the complete solution

```
! Sieve of Eratosthenes
write "Input highest number :- "
let n = readi
let p = vector 2::n of true
for i = 2 to truncate( sqrt( n ) ) do
if p( i ) do
for j = 2 * i to n by i do p( j ) := false
write "The primes less than ",n : 4," are :-'n"
let format.control := 0
for i = 2 to n do
if p( i ) do
begin
    write i : 5
    format.control := format.control + 1
    if format.control = 8 do { write "'n" ; format.control := 0 }
end
?
```

The above problem was so simple that we did not need to use any procedures in its solution.

Consider next the problem of writing a general purpose procedure for evaluating the integral of an arbitrary function f(x)

between limits a and b. Since we do not know the explicit function to be integrated and do not want to have to pass its values either singly or as a vector from the calling program we must use the idea of a procedure as a parameter of another procedure. Such a parameter will be declared along with the other parameters in the procedure declaration. This requires some specification of the 'shape', or more formally the type, of this parameter. Note that f(x) is a function with one real parameter x and on evaluation produces a real result. We use the notation

   (**real** -> **real**)f

as the required formal parameter declaration in the procedure heading. This is included amongst the parameters in exactly the same way as other formal parameters such as **int** i, **real** u and so on. The notation (**real** -> **real**) thus corresponds exactly to a type declaration such as **int** or **real** and is indeed the 'type' of this parameter. Note that we only name the object of this type and do not name the constituents of its type declaration. This is because we only need to declare the types themselves and at this stage are not concerned with their actual existence. We can now write down our declaration of the procedure heading as

procedure integral((**real** -> **real**)f
     real a,b ; **cint** no.of.steps -> **real**)

  Since we do not wish to discuss the intricacies of sophisticated numerical techniques we will use the trapezoidal rule to perform the integration but this can easily be replaced by other numerical integration methods.

  The required formula to approximate the integral of function f between a and b is

0.5 * h * (f(a) + 2 * (f(a+h) + ... + f(a + (no.of.steps-1) * h)) + f(b))

where h = (b-a)/no.of.steps.

  To simplify the computation slightly we rearrange this as

h * (0.5 * f(a) + f(a+h) + ... + f(a+(no.of.steps-1) * h) + 0.5 * f(b))

We can now write the complete procedure as

procedure integral((**real** -> **real**)f

```
                    real a,b ; cint no.of.steps -> real )
begin
    let h = ( b - a ) / no.of.steps
    let sum := 0.5 * ( f( a ) + f( b ) )
    for i = 1 to no.of.steps - 1 do
    begin
        a := a + h
        sum := sum + f( a )
    end
    h * sum
end
```

A call of this procedure to integrate sin(x) between 0 and pi using 10 steps, and to put the result in y, may be written

```
y := integral( sin,0,pi,10 )
```

Notice that we just write sin and not sin(x) since we are passing the sin function and not a value of sin(x) as a parameter.

The function sin can be replaced by any other function in the program such as

```
procedure quadratic( real x -> real )
( 3 * x + 4 ) * x - 1
```

with a corresponding call

```
integral( quadratic,1,4,30 )
```

We can now use this single variable integral to evaluate a double integral of a function g(x,y) where x goes from a to b and y goes from c to d.

In order to do this we will write a procedure with name double.integral which will integrate f(x,y) in the y-direction for each value of x and then integrate this new function with respect to x. We cannot use the integral procedure twice over directly since g is a function of two variables whereas f is a function of one variable. We overcome this by defining a new function G which is f with the x value held constant. A procedure to do this could be

```
procedure double.integral( ( real,real -> real )g
                    creal a,b,c,d ; cint x.steps,y.steps -> real )
begin
    let x.coord := a
    procedure G( real y -> real ) ; g( x.coord,y )
    let hx = ( b - a ) / x.steps
    let double.sum := 0.5 * integral( G,c,d,y.steps )
    for i = 1 to x.steps - 1 do
    begin
        x.coord := x.coord + hx
        double.sum := double.sum + integral( G,c,d,y.steps )
    end
    x.coord := b
    hx * ( double.sum + 0.5 * integral( G,c,d,y.steps ) )
end
```

This uses the procedure integral as defined above.

A typical call of this procedure using a previously defined function h(x,y) could be

double.integral(h,0,1,0,2,20,40)

A more sophisticated example for the evaluation of a double integral is given in the examples at the end of this chapter.

Consider next the well known problem of the Towers of Hanoi. A fuller discussion of this problem is given in Cole (1981) and in Rouse Ball (1896) so we will restrict ourselves to the following brief description.

Three pegs labelled a, b, c exist and on one of them, say a, are placed n disks in descending order of size with the largest at the bottom and the smallest at the top. The other two pegs are initially empty. The problem is to move the disks to another peg, say b, but only moving the disks one at a time and at no time placing a larger disk on top of a smaller one.

This is a good example of a problem in which one needs to think carefully before writing a word of code. If we only have one disk then the problem is trivial. We simply move that disk from a to b and are finished. Indeed if we have no disks at all the solution is even simpler.

We do nothing and the problems is solved! If n > 0 then some thought leads us to the idea that if we can find a way to move, according to the rules, the top n-1 disks to peg c leaving the largest on peg a, then we may move this larger disk from a to b and never move it again. We now have almost exactly the same problem as before, but have to move the disks from peg c to peg b with the vital difference that we have only to move n-1 disks instead of n. Such a solution, expressing a computational step in terms of itself, is said to be recursive. It leads to a solution because of the special cases n=1 and n=0.

The three steps required in the above solution are

   (i)   move n-1 disks from a to c
  (ii)   move 1 disk from a to b
 (iii)   move n-1 disks from c to b

This transforms immediately into the recursive procedure

```
procedure hanoi( cint n ; cstring a,b,c )
if n > 0 do
begin
     hanoi( n-1,a,c,b )
     move( a,b )
     hanoi( n-1,c,b,a )
end
```

where n is the number of disks and the strings a, b and c are the names of the pegs. The procedure move is simply a clause to write out the move of a single disk

```
procedure move( cstring a,b )
write a,"->",b,"´n"
```

The complete program with a typical call is now as follows:

```
!Towers of Hanoi
procedure move( cstring a,b )
write a,"->",b,"´n"
procedure hanoi( cint n ; cstring a,b,c )
```

```
if n > 0 do
begin
    hanoi( n-1,a,c,b )
    move( a,b )
    hanoi( n-1,c,b,a )
end
hanoi( 9,"a","b","c" )
?
```

Try working this through but with n = 3 or 4 to understand exactly how it works.

Recursive solutions to problems are often criticised as being only of interest to the academics and not very practical. This is certainly not true and there are many problems which yield elegantly and efficiently to recursive methods. Two such methods are the sorting algorithms known as treesort which you saw in Chapter 10 and quicksort which we discuss here. The bubblesort method discussed earlier is of order n squared in the sense that the time taken in general to produce a solution increases as the square of the number of elements n. The reason for this is that in finding the biggest element in one scan we accumulate no further information about the remaining elements. The quicksort algorithm is aimed at gaining information at every stage about the relative size of elements and using this information to reduce the computation time to the order of n * log(n).

The technique is to choose a starting element arbitrarily and then by scanning inwards from both ends of the vector simultaneously, to split it into two parts, the one on the left having values less than or equal to the chosen element. The one on the right has values greater than or equal to it. We can then apply the algorithm to the two parts quite independently of each other. The reason for this technique being in general much faster than bubblesort is that the number of elements in each part is usually nearer to 0.5n than to n-1. One can of course produce pathological examples where this does not happen but in practice this seldom occurs. Methods of speeding up the algorithm still further will be discussed in the examples at the end of this chapter.

Procedure quicksort will have as parameters a vector of values x to be sorted and two integer variables lbd and ubd which delimit initially the part of x currently being sorted. These are not equal in general to **lwb**(x) and **upb**(x).

We will arbitrarily choose the value, 'split.val' for the splitting comparisons to be the value of the element with index (lb + ub) **div** 2. An improvement on this choice will be given as an exercise. As an example consider the values

        3   9   4   6   7   8   5   2

in a vector with indices from 1 to 8. The split point chosen will be in position 4 and this has value 6. The aim now is to split the vector into two parts with the left hand part having elements with values less than or equal to split.val and the right hand part having elements greater than or equal to split.val. This is done by scanning in from the left and right and looking for elements which are out of place in this scheme. If such a pair is found then they are swapped and the process continues until the left and right hand scans meet. In general this will not be at the previously chosen split point but this does not matter since the element there has not been moved.

while lb < ub **do**
begin
    while lb < ub **and** x(lb) $\leq$ split.val **do** lb := lb + 1
    while lb < ub **and** x(ub) $\geq$ split.val **do** ub := ub - 1
    if lb < ub **do**
    begin
        swap(x,lb,ub)
        lb := lb + 1
        if lb < ub **do** ub := ub - 1
    end
end

In the above example the first pair of values to be swapped is 9 and 2 and then 7 and 5. The scans finally meet at the element with value 8. The order of the elements will now be

        3   2   4   6   5   8   7   9

with the final split point being at position 6. We now split the vector into two parts with the value in the position where the scan meets being included with the right or left part depending on whether or not it is greater or less than the old split value itself. Sometimes the split value will be by chance in the position where the two pointers meet and in this case it does not need to be included in either subvector. We must always ensure that lb and ub do not go outside the range from lbd to ubd. The piece of program to do this is written below immediately after the completion of the splitting code. Finally we make recursive calls of quicksort on the resulting pair of subvectors only finishing when a subvector is of length 1. The first split for the above example will be into the subvectors

        3   2   4   6   5

and

        8   7   9

The complete program including the swap procedure is therefore

```
procedure swap( *int x ; cint i,j )
begin
    let temp = x( i )
    x( i ) := x( j )
    x( j ) := temp
end
procedure quicksort( *int x ; cint lbd,ubd )
begin
    let lb := lbd ; let ub := ubd
    let split.val = x( ( lb + ub ) div 2 )
    while lb < ub do
    begin
        while lb < ub and x( lb ) ≤ split.val do lb := lb + 1
        while lb < ub and x( ub ) ≥ split.val do ub := ub - 1
        if lb < ub do
        begin
            swap( x,lb,ub )
            lb := lb + 1
            ub := ub - 1
```

```
              end
           end
        ub := lb     ! ub may have passed lb
        let val = x( lb )       !To reduce indexing time
        case true of
        val > split.val   : lb := lb - 1
        val < split.val   : ub := ub + 1
        default           : begin
                              ub := ub + 1
                              lb := lb - 1
                            end
        if lbd < lb do quicksort( x,lbd,lb )
        if ub < ubd do quicksort( x,ub,ubd )
end
```

Exercises 12

12.1 Write down formal parameters to be used in a procedure heading corresponding to the following procedures.

   (i)   **procedure** f(**real** x ; **int** i -> **real**)
   (ii) **procedure** g(** **real** x, y ; **int** -> * **real**)
   (iii) **procedure** h(**real** x, y ; (**real**, **int** -> **real**) f -> **string**)
   (iv) **procedure** p(**bool** b -> **bool**)

12.2 Primes frequently occur in pairs p, p+2 and less frequently in triples q, q+2, q+6. For example, 11, 13 and 29, 31 are examples of prime pairs and 5, 7, 11 and 17, 19, 23 are examples of prime triples. Write a program to list

   (i)   all prime pairs from 3 up to some integer n
   (ii) all prime triples from 3 up to some integer n
   (iii) all prime pairs and triples from 3 up to some integer n but
         excluding those prime pairs which are part of a triple.

12.3 Write a piece of program to integrate the function x * ln(x) from x=1 to 2 using (i) 10 steps (ii) 20 steps. Compare your answers with the exact integral of this function.

12.4 Determine the effect of the following program

```
procedure integral( ( real -> real ) F ; creal a,b -> real )
( b - a ) * F( ( a + b ) / 2.0 )
procedure G( real z -> real )
begin
     procedure ep( creal y -> real ) ; exp( z * y )
     integral( ep,3.0,4.0 )
end
write fformat( integral( G,1.0,2.0 ),4,2 ),"'n"
?
```

12.5 The procedure quicksort can be improved in the following two ways.

    (i) by making a special case when the number of terms to be sorted is 2.

    (ii) by choosing the split value to be the middle value of x(lb), x(lb + ub) div 2, x(ub).

Modify the quicksort program to incorporate these two improvements.

Solutions to Exercises 12

12.1
    (i) (real,int -> real) p
    (ii) (**real,**real,int -> *real) q
    (iii) (real,real,(real,int -> real) -> string) s
    (iv) (bool -> bool) t

12.2 Use the Sieve of Eratosthenes program replacing the **write** clause by the following :

```
write "Table of prime pairs'n'n"
let i := 3
while i <= n - 2 do
begin
    if p( i ) and p( i + 2 ) do
    write i : 6,i + 2 : 6,"'n"
    i := i + 2
end
write "Table of prime triples'n'n"
let j := 3
while j <= n - 6 do
```

```
if p( j ) and p( j + 2 ) and p( j + 6 ) then
begin
    write j : 6,j + 2 : 6,j + 6 : 6,"'n"
    j := j + 6
end else j := j + 2
write "Table of triples and pairs not in triples'n'n"
let k := 3
while k ≤ n - 6 do
if p( k ) and p( k + 2 ) and p( k + 6 ) then
begin
    write k : 6,k + 2 : 6,k + 6 : 6,"'n"
    k := k + 6
end else
begin
    if p( k ) and p( k + 2 ) do
    write k : 6,k + 2 : 6,"'n"
    k := k + 2
end
if k ≤ n - 2 and p( k ) and p( k + 2 ) do
write k : 6,k + 2 : 6,"'n"
```

12.3 We need to write a procedure corresponding to the required function and also a call of the 'integral' procedure. The following will do

```
procedure f( real x -> real )
x * ln( x )
write "The integral with 10 steps is " ,integral( f,1,2,10 ) ,"'n",
    "The integral with 20 steps is ",integral( f ,1 ,2 ,20 )
```

12.4 The procedure 'integral' in this example computes a simple integral with one variable in one step using the mid-point rule. The type of the procedure G is (**real -> real**) and is therefore a valid parameter of the procedure 'integral'. The call

           integral(G1,2)

gives the integral of G from 1 to 2. That is, the integral from 1 to 2 of the integral from 3 to 4 of the function exp(x*y).

12.5 (i) This requires only a trivial modification to swap the two elements if necessary. The first four lines of executable code after procedure swap below will do this.

(ii) The difficulty here is to distinguish efficiently between the six cases

$a \leq b \leq c$

$c \leq a \leq b$

$a \leq c \leq b$

$b \leq a \leq c$

$c \leq b \leq a$

$b \leq c \leq a$

and to take appropriate action. The case required can be determined by using an **if** and **case** clauses as below. The action within each case is to rearrange, if necessary, the values in x(lbd), x(ubd) and x(split.pt). The procedure can terminate if there are only three values to be sorted. This case is covered by changing the test at the start of the main final loop to

if ubd > lbd + 2

If this test succeeds sorting can continue with both upper and lower bounds moved inwards by one place. The new quicksort procedure is as follows.

```
procedure quicksort( * int x ; cint lbd,ubd )
begin
    procedure swap( *int x ; cint i,j )
    { let temp = x( i ) ; x( i ) := x( j ) ; x( j ) := temp }

    let a = x( lbd ) ; let c = x( ubd )
    if ubd = lbd + 1
    then if a > c do { x( lbd ) := c ; x( ubd ) := a }
    else
    begin
        let split.pt = ( lbd + ubd ) div 2
        let b = x( split.pt )
        let split.val = if a ≤ b then
        case true of
        b ≤ c  : b
        c ≤ a  : { x( split.pt ) := a; x( lbd ) := c; x( ubd ) := b; a }
```

```
            default: { x( split.pt ) := c ; x( ubd ) := b ; c}
        else
        case true of
        a ≤ c   : { x( split.pt ) := a ; x( lbd ) := b ; a }
        c ≤ b   : { x( lbd ) := c ; x( ubd ) := a ; b }
        default: { x( lbd ) := b; x( split.pt ) := a; x( ubd ) := a; c }
        if ubd > lbd + 2 do
        begin
            let lb := lbd + 1 ; let ub := ubd - 1
            while lb < ub do
            begin
                while lb < ub and x( lb ) ≤ split.val do lb := lb + 1
                while lb < ub and x( ub ) ≥ split.val do ub := ub - 1
                if lb < ub do
                begin
                    swap( x,lb,ub )
                    lb := lb + 1
                    ub := ub - 1
                end
            end
            ub := lb     ! ub may have passed lb
            let val = x( lb )        !To reduce indexing time
            case true of
            val > split.val  : lb := lb - 1
            val < split.val  : ub := ub + 1
            default          : begin
                                    ub := ub + 1
                                    lb := lb - 1
                               end
            if lbd < lb do quicksort( x,lbd,lb )
            if ub < ubd do quicksort( x,ub,ubd )
        end
    end
end
```

13 BACKTRACKING PROBLEMS

One particular class of problems that is of special interest is the backtracking class. Solutions to these problems proceed on a trial and error basis. When a possible solution is found to be in error we backtrack and try another. The problems that can be solved in this manner are very often combinatorial in nature.

Generally, the number of paths that can be taken is very large and can only be limited by a heuristic approach. Loosely speaking, a heuristic approach is one which gives a good chance of success at finding a solution without any guarantee that it will succeed. We will not discuss general heuristics here but concentrate on a technique for solving backtracking problems. The heuristic, if necessary, can be fitted at a later stage. The method of solution is the one introduced earlier of successively refining the problem into sub-problems until a solution is arrived at.

13.1 Repeated substring problem

Let a string be called acceptable if it contains no pair of identical adjacent substrings.
e.g.

  A AB ABA ABACA

are acceptable but

  AA ABB ABABC

are not since they have repeated adjacent substrings. Note that in the general case the adjacent substrings may be of arbitrary length. If we are restricted to using only two different letters then the longest possible string is

  ABA

However, with three letters it can be proved that there exist arbitrarily long acceptable strings. The problem is to write a program to find an acceptable string of a given length for three letters.

This is a typical backtracking problem and if you think it is simple try doing it by hand for a string of length 12 say. As with any problem we must decide on the representation of the data. In this problem we require a string and an integer to tell us how many valid characters we have in the string. We will use the three letters A,B and C. The solution progresses like this. Add a new letter, an A, to the string ; if this is not acceptable alter it to B and if this is not acceptable alter it to C. If this is not acceptable we have an invalid string and we must backtrack altering the previous letter in the string until it is acceptable again and then carry on. This, of course, is recursive. Every time we have an acceptable string we add a letter until the string is of the correct length.

Let us write the main program

```
let s := ""            !This will hold the string
let n := 0             !This is the number of valid characters so far
write "Input string length "
let lnth = readi
while n ≠ lnth do
begin
     add.a.letter
     while ~acceptable do alter
end
write "An acceptable string of length ",lnth," is ",s,"'n" ?
```

This is a very simple program in which we have invented 3 procedures to add a letter to the string, to test whether it is acceptable and to alter the string if necessary. You should convince yourself that this program is correct before going on.

We will now write the procedure to add a letter.

procedure add.a.letter ; { s := s ++ "A" ; n := n + 1 }

This adds an 'A' to the end of the string and increments the number of characters by one.

The next procedure to write is the one which alters the letter if it is not valid. The procedure alters 'A' to 'B' or 'B' to 'C'. If the letter is already 'C' we must backtrack. To do this we subtract 1 from the number of valid characters and call the procedure itself to deal with the situation for n-1 characters.

procedure alter
case s(n|1) **of**
"A"   : s := s(1|n - 1) ++ "B"
"B"   : s := s(1|n - 1) ++ "C"
default : { n := n - 1 ; alter }

All that is left is to write the procedure to test the acceptability of the string. This will only be tested when we add a letter or alter previous ones. Therefore we do not require to test all the substrings. If our string so far is of length n, then the first n-1 letters are acceptable from the way in which we built it up. We need only test the effect of the last character on the string by testing all the substrings that it may appear in. The following procedure will do. (You should check this for yourself with say n = 5).

procedure acceptable(-> **bool**)
begin
    let ok := **true** ; **let** p := 1
    while ok **and** p $\leq$ n **div** 2 **do**
    begin
        ok := s(n - p + 1|p) $\neq$ s(n - 2 * p + 1|p)
        p := p + 1
    end
    ok
end

Putting the pieces together gives us the complete program. However there is still one problem. The solution assumes that there is an acceptable string of length 'lnth'. If there is not we will backtrack too far and eventually have a string indexing error. Therefore we must change the program slightly to take account of this.

To ensure that we do not backtrack too far we introduce a boolean variable 'more' which is initially **true**. This variable is declared as **true** but will be set to **false** if we attempt to backtrack too far and the main program controlling loops must make use of this. To set the variable we must change the procedure alter.

```
procedure alter
case s( n|1 ) of
"A"     : s := s( 1|n-1 ) ++ "B"
"B"     : s := s( 1|n-1 ) ++ "C"
default : { n := n - 1 ; if n = 0 then more := false else alter }
```

The only alteration is that before backtracking we test to see if it is possible to backtrack and if not we set the boolean variable to **false**. We must now alter the main program as well.

```
!                 Main Program
write "Input string length "
let lnth = readi
let n := 0 ; let s := "" ; let more := true
while more and n < lnth do
begin
    add.a.letter
    while more and ~acceptable do alter
end
if more then write "An acceptable string of length ",lnth," is ",s,"'n"
        else write "There is no acceptable string of length ",lnth,"'n"
?
```

Finally we may refine the solution to find **all** the acceptable strings of a given length simply by changing the main program. This gives the final solution

```
!Program to find all the acceptable strings of length lnth
let s := "" ; let n := 0 ; let more := true
procedure add.a.letter ; { s := s ++ "A" ; n := n + 1 }
```

```
procedure alter
case s( n|1 ) of
"A"     : s := s( 1|n-1 ) ++ "B"
"B"     : s := s( 1|n-1 ) ++ "C"
default : { n := n - 1 ; if n = 0 then more := false else alter }
procedure acceptable( -> bool )
begin
     let ok := true ; let p := 1
     while ok and p ≤ n div 2 do
     begin
          ok := s( n - p + 1|p ) ≠ s( n - 2 * p + 1|p )
          p := p + 1
     end
     ok
end
!                  Main Program
write "Input string length "
let lnth = readi ; let count := 0
while more and n ≤ lnth do
begin
     if n = lnth then alter else add.a.letter
     while more and ~acceptable do alter
     if n = lnth do { write "An acceptable string is ",s,"´n"
                      count := count + 1 }
end
if more then write "Total number of strings of length ",
                    lnth : 3," is ",count : 4,"´n"
        else write "There is no acceptable string of length ",
                    lnth : 4,"´n"
?
```

13.2 Knight's tour

The knight's tour problem is another well known backtracking problem. A knight is placed on an n x n board and is allowed to move according to the rules of chess. The problem is to compute a tour of the board in which every square is visited once and only once.

A method of solution to this problem is as follows. From the initial position select a legal move and continue to select legal moves until it is no longer possible to do so. At this point we have either filled the board, in which case we have a solution, or we have to backtrack one move at a time until a solution is found or we find that none exists. You should be warned that this problem can easily take vast amounts of computation time and should not be attempted without the further aid of a heuristic algorithm. The first attempt at the program which includes a lot of procedures to be written later could be

```
initialise
while board.not.full do
begin
     add.knight
     while ~acceptable do alter
end
print.solution
?
```

Note how similar this looks to the previous program.
We can immediately refine this solution to make sure that we do not backtrack too far. As in the string problem we will use a boolean variable to control this. The program now becomes

```
initialise
while more and board.not.full do
begin
     add.knight
     while more and ~acceptable do alter
end
if more then print.solution
        else write "No solution exists'n"
?
```

We must now choose the representation of the information we require to solve the problem. To represent the board we will use an n x n vector

let board = **vector** 1::n,1::n **of** 0

where   board(x,y) = 0   means field(x,y) has not been visited
and   board(x,y) = i   where i ≠ 0 means it has

Since we know that this is a backtracking solution we also know that we have to be able to get back to the previous move. We will use the values in board to do this. At the end of the program we will have a solution on the board which is a backward thread of the moves. This can then be followed to put in the correct move numbers.

Given a starting pair of co-ordinates (x,y) there are at most eight possible moves to reach the destination (new.x,new.y). They are numbered from 1 to 8 although all are not always permissible.

	3		2	
4				1
		K		
5				8
	6		7	

The problem is solved by trying each of the 8 positions in turn at each stage until one is found to be acceptable. If none are acceptable we must backtrack. (new.x,new.y) can be found from (x,y) by adding the differences of the co-ordinates. This is done by using the two vectors

let a = @1 **of cint**[2,1,-1,-2,-2,-1,1,2]
let b = @1 **of cint**[1,2,2,1,-1,-2,-2,-1]

and using an index 'index' to denote which move of the 8 we are trying. So

new.x := x + a(index)
new.y := y + b(index)

It can now be seen that

board(x,y)

denotes the value of index used to move to this position. We can therefore subtract the values in a and b from x and y to return to the previous position. One consequence of this is a slight alteration to the main program in which we work on the proposed move until it is acceptable and then add the knight. The main program is then

```
write "Input board size "
let n = readi ; let n.squared = n * n
let a = @1 of cint[ 2,1,-1,-2,-2,-1,1,2 ]
let b = @1 of cint[ 1,2,2,1,-1,-2,-2,-1 ]
let board = vector 1::n,1::n of 0
let x := 1 ; let y := 1    !starting position with no loss of generality
let new.x := 1 ; let new.y := 1
let index := 1 ; let count := 1
let more := true
!      Main Program
board( x,y ) := 1
while more and count < n.squared do
begin
     select.new.move
     while more and ~acceptable do alter
     add.knight
end
if more then { sort.board ; print.board }
        else write "No solution exists'n"
?
```

We can easily fill in some of these procedures.

```
procedure select.new.move
{ new.x := x + a( index ) ; new.y := y + b( index ) }
```

This we have seen before. For a move to be acceptable it must be on the board and the proposed square must not be occupied. Notice that we are testing the new move for acceptability.

```
procedure acceptable( -> bool )
new.x ≤ n and new.x ≥ 1 and new.y ≤ n and new.y ≥ 1 and
board( new.x,new.y ) = 0
```

Adding a knight to the board entails updating the counts and the board with the index of the acceptable move.

procedure add.knight
begin
    x := new.x ; y := new.y
    board(x,y) := index
    index := 1 ; count := count + 1
end

We are now ready to write the procedure alter. This normally steps through all the moves by incrementing index and selecting a new move. If all the moves are exhausted we must backtrack if possible.

procedure alter
if index = 8 **then**
begin
    count := count - 1
    index := board(x,y)
    board(x,y) := 0
    x := x - a(index) ; y := y - b(index)
    if count = 0 **then** more := **false else** alter
end else { index := index + 1 ; select.new.move }

Notice in particular the steps required to undo a move. The count is decremented, the board position is set to 0, the old position is calculated and backtracking is performed if possible.

This is enough to perform the calculation. We require a procedure to thread its way backwards through the board replacing the entry with the number of the move.

procedure sort.board
for i = n.squared **to** 2 **by** -1 **do**
begin
    let j = board(x,y)
    board(x,y) := i
    x := x - a(j) ; y := y - b(j)

end

and a procedure to print the result.

procedure print.board
for i = 1 **to** n **do**
begin
    for j = 1 **to** n **do write** board(i,j) : 3
    write "'n"
end

    Putting the whole program together gives

let n = **readi** ; **let** n.squared = n * n
let a = @1 **of cint**[2,1,-1,-2,-2,-1,1,2]
let b = @1 **of cint**[1,2,2,1,-1,-2,-2,-1]
let board = **vector** 1::n,1::n **of** 0
let x := 1 ; **let** y := 1   !starting position with no loss of generality
let new.x := 1 ; **let** new.y := 1
let index := 1 ; **let** count := 1
let more := **true**
procedure select.new.move
{ new.x := x + a(index) ; new.y := y + b(index) }
procedure acceptable(-> **bool**)
new.x $\leq$ n **and** new.x $\geq$ 1 **and** new.y $\leq$ n **and** new.y $\geq$ 1 **and**
board(new.x,new.y) = 0
procedure alter
if index = 8 **then**
begin
    count := count - 1
    index := board(x,y)
    board(x,y) := 0
    x := x - a(index) ; y := y - b(index)
    if count = 0 **then** more := **false else** alter
end else { index := index + 1 ; select.new.move }
procedure add.knight
begin

```
        x := new.x ; y := new.y
        board( x,y ) := index
        index := 1 ; count := count + 1
end
procedure sort.board
for i = n.squared to 2 by -1 do
begin
        let j = board( x,y )
        board( x,y ) := i
        x := x - a( j ) ; y := y - b( j )
end
procedure print.board
for i = 1 to n do
begin
        for j = 1 to n do write board( i,j ) : 3
        write "'n"
end
!       Main Program
board( x,y ) := 1
while more and count < n.squared do
begin
        select.new.move
        while more and ~acceptable do alter
        add.knight
end
if more then { sort.board ; print.board }
        else write "No solution exists'n"
?
```

This program should not be run on a computer without the use of a heuristic. The heuristic can be fitted in by changing the acceptability test or the select next move procedure. We do not wish to consider the theory of heuristics here - it would take another book to do so. However, you might try one for yourself. How about trying to move towards the centre of the board if possible. Do not forget to put a time limit on your program as you may waste enormous amounts of computer time. The first solution that this program would give on a 5 x 5 board is

```
 1   6  15  10  21
14   9  20   5  16
19   2   7  22  11
 8  13  24  17   4
25  18   3  12  23
```

It is left as an exercise to extend the program to find all the solutions.

Exercises 13

13.1 Write a program to place 8 queens on a chess board so that no queen threatens another according to the rules of chess. The solution will backtrack.

13.2 Modify your program to find all the solutions to the 8 queens problem.

Solutions to Exercises 13

13.1
! Program to place 8 queens on a chess board
let n := 0 ; **let** more := **true**
let pos = **vector** 1::8 **of** 0
procedure add.a.queen ; { n := n + 1 ; pos(n) := 1 }
procedure alter
if pos(n) = 8 **then**
begin
    n := n - 1
    if n = 0 **then** more := **false else** alter
end else pos(n) := pos(n) + 1
procedure cantake(**cint** i,j -> **bool**)
pos(i) = pos(j) **or**
abs(pos(i) - pos(j)) = abs(i - j)
procedure incheck(-> **bool**)
begin
    let check := **false** ; **let** i := 1
    while i < n **and** ~check **do**
    begin
        if cantake(i,n) **do** check := **true**

```
                i := i + 1
        end
        check
end
!*********** Main Program ***************
while more and n < 8 do
begin
        add.a.queen
        while more and incheck do alter
end
if ~more then
begin
        write "The solution to the 8 queens problem is'n"
        for i = 1 to 8 do write pos( i ) : 3
end else write "No solution exists'n"
?

13.2
! Program to place 8 queens on a chess board
! and find all the solutions
let n := 0 ; let more := true ; let count := 0
let pos = vector 1::8 of 0
procedure add.a.queen ; { n := n + 1 ; pos( n ) := 1 }
procedure alter
if pos( n ) = 8 then
begin
        n := n - 1
        if n = 0 then more := false else alter
end else pos( n ) := pos( n ) + 1
procedure cantake( cint i,j -> bool )
( pos( i ) = pos( j ) ) or
( abs( pos( i ) - pos( j ) ) = abs( i - j ) )
procedure incheck( -> bool )
begin
        let check := false ; let i := 1
        while i < n and ~check do
        begin
                if cantake( i,n ) do check := true
```

```
            i := i + 1
        end
        check
end
!*********** Main Program ***************
while more and n ≤ 8 do
begin
        if n = 8 then alter else add.a.queen
        while more and incheck do alter
        if n = 8 do
        begin
            write "A solution to the 8 queens problem is "
            for i = 1 to 8 do write pos( i ) : 3
            write "'n"
            count := count + 1
        end
end
if ~more then
begin
        write "The number of solutions to the 8 queens problem is ",
            count : 4
end else write "No solution exists'n"
?
```

14 OUTLINE GRAPHICS

Any graphics facility is more directly dependent on hardware than the conventional arithmetic and data manipulation properties of computer languages. For this reason, there is a different implementation of the S-algol system for each hardware configuration so if you want to use the graphics constructions in S-algol you will need to have both the hardware and corresponding compiler version.

Even without this it is interesting to investigate how a language such as S-algol can incorporate a graphics capability which is in harmony with the design principles of the rest of the language and we therefore give a brief description of graphics in S-algol.

The S-algol graphics facility is called Outline Morrison (1982c) and it provides an infinite two dimensional real space in which abstract pictures made up of lines and points may be drawn. Altering the relationship between different parts of an abstract picture is performed by geometric transformation. This means that pictures are usually built up of sub-pictures. The abstract description of a picture is independent of how it is drawn and the two concepts are kept separate.

The language requirements fall into two parts, namely the logical facilities for describing line drawings and the physical attributes for drawing them.

The first requirement is for a data type **pic** which allows descriptions of pictures to be made and named. Like all other data objects in S-algol, pictures have full 'civil rights' which means that there are objects of type **pic**, **pic** expressions, vectors of **pic**, **pic** procedures and so on.

The simplest object of type **pic** is the point and this is defined to be a pair of reals enclosed in square brackets. Thus the expression

[0.1,2.0]

is a picture representing the point with Cartesian coordinates 0.1, 2.0. It may be declared by a declaration such as

let point = [0.1,2.0]

or

let another.point := [3,2.5]

with the usual S-algol conventions.

Pictures may be joined together using the join operator '^'. Thus the assignment clause

another.point := point ^ another.point

describes the line joining [0.1,2.0] to [3,2.5].

It is immediately obvious that some ordering of points in pictures must be defined so that we can unambiguously determine which point in the first picture is joined to which point in the second. The points in pictures are implicitly ordered by the inductive rule that if A and B are the first and last points of picture p and C and D are the first and last points of picture q then

p ^ q

is the picture formed by joining p to q by a line BC and the resulting picture has first point A and last point D.

Thus if a and b are two open sided rectangles defined by

let a = [3,2] ^ [3,4] ^ [12,4] ^ [12,2]
let b = [3,-1] ^ [3,-3] ^ [12,-3] ^ [12,-1]

then

let c := a ^ b

defines a new picture with start point [3,2], finish point [12,-1] and consisting of a and b joined by a line from [12,2] to [3,-1]. Try drawing the two pictures yourself to see exactly what this means.

It is also useful to be able to combine two pictures **without** joining them with a line. The operator '&' is used for this operation. Thus

>   **let** d := a & b

defines a composite picture of two open sided rectangles, this time not joined by a line from [12,2] to [3,-1] but still having the start point [3,2] and finish point [12,-1].

There are three basic operators which may be applied to an object p of type **pic**. These are

scale p **by** a,b
shift p **by** c,d
rotate p **by** e

where a, b, c, d, e are objects of type **real**. It should be obvious that **scale** changes the scale of p by factors a and b in the x and y direction respectively. Note that

>   **scale** p **by** -1,-1

reflects the picture p in the origin of coordinates and

>   **scale** p **by** -1,1

reflects p in the y-axis. Similarly **shift** has the effect of adding c to all x and adding d to all y coordinates in the picture.

>   **rotate** p **by** e

rotates p clockwise through e degrees about the origin of coordinates. Note that the angle is in degrees not radians. To rotate a picture q about a point [s,t] without ultimately changing the origin of coordinates, it is necessary to shift the origin to [s,t], perform the necessary rotation and then reverse the first translation of coordinates. Since pictures are first class citizens we can write a procedure to do this and produce the result as its value.

procedure rotate.about.point(**pic** p ; **real** s,t,theta -> **pic**)
shift rotate shift p **by** -s,-t **by** theta **by** s,t

This could have been broken down into a three clause sequence

let q := **shift** p **by** -s,-t
q := **rotate** q **by** theta
shift q **by** s,t

but as written above it illustrates the generality of the data type **pic**.

Strings may be written anywhere in a picture by using

> **text** s **from** x,y **to** r,s

where s is any string and x, y and r, s are the coordinates of the start and end points of the position where the string is to be placed. The string characters will be scaled and the whole string rotated if necessary to fit between the specified points. Thus

> **text** "upside down" **from** 10,1 **to** 0,1

would result in "upside down" being written upside down. Since all pictures will ultimately be drawn as collections of dots, it may be that text will be distorted by unsuitable choice of the end points. Clearly this is dependent on the resolution of the output device so general rules other than 'suck it and see' cannot be given.

Pictures may be coloured. Thus

> p := **colour** q **in** "white"

will assign to p the picture q coloured in white. The relevance of colouring is dependent on the output device available. In implementations where full colour is not available the picture will eventually be drawn as best it can. In a full colour system the sequence

```
let square = [ 1,1 ] ^ [ 1,-1 ] ^ [ -1,-1 ] ^ [ -1,1 ] ^ [ 1,1 ]
let double.square = colour square in "red" &
                    colour rotate square by 45 in "blue"
```

defines a red square with a blue square rotated through 45 degrees superimposed.

Another hardware feature common to all graphics implementations is the facility to clear the screen. Thus the command

> erase.to("black")

clears the screen to the background colour black. Again the interpretation of this command depends on the availability of a colour system.

In order to draw a picture, the lines that make up the picture must be mapped onto the output device. Since abstract pictures are defined in an infinite two dimensional space, the user must provide a window on the space which defines that part of the picture to be drawn. For example,

      draw(box,-3.0,3.0,-3.0,3.0)

would draw everything in the picture 'box' that lies in the coordinate space between -3 to 3 in the x direction and -3 to 3 in the y direction.

      Note that draw does not alter what is already displayed and can therefore be used to superimpose pictures if required. This may be necessary because of storage constraints if the picture becomes too complex to represent as a single one.

      For the purposes of drawing, a picture will be mapped on to the part of the screen defined by the variables

      scrn.x.min scrn.x.max scrn.y.min scrn.y.max

which are initially set by the system to define the whole screen. However the user may wish the picture to be drawn on a particular section of the screen and the command split.screen is defined for this. For example

split.screen(scrn.x.min,(scrn.x.min + scrn.x.max) **div** 2,
            scrn.y.min,(scrn.y.min + scrn.y.max) **div** 2)

followed by a draw command would draw the picture in the bottom left hand quarter of the screen. The actual default values of scrn.x.min etc. will depend on the device being used.

      We continue this chapter with a few examples. The first of these is to define a square and then to build up a composite picture consisting of the square rotated by 0, 11.25, 22.5, 33.75, 45.00,..., 78.75 degrees. Finally, the composite picture will be drawn to fill the whole screen and also part of the screen inside the first picture.

      We first define the initial square by

let initial.square = [1,1] ^ [1,-1] ^ [-1,-1] ^ [-1,1] ^ [1,1]

We now build up the composite abstract picture using the '&' operator and **rotate**.

let squares := initial.square
for i = 1 **to** 7 **do**
squares := squares & **rotate** initial.square **by** i * 11.25

      We immediately notice that we can improve this piece of

program to give a result of computational complexity log(n) rather than the number of rotations n by rotating the composite picture at each step rather than just rotating the original square.

let squares := initial.square
let rotation = 11.25 ; **let** i := 1
while i ≤ 4 **do**
begin
    squares := squares & **rotate** squares **by** rotation * i
    i := i + i
end

We now have only to draw the picture twice. The first can be done by the command

        draw(squares,-1.5,1.5,-1.5,1.5)

The second can be done either by suitably enlarging the 'draw' parameters or by suitably splitting the screen. We can thus use either

        draw(squares,-2.6,2.6,-2.6,2.6)

or on a 256 * 256 dot screen

        split.screen(55,200,55,200)
        draw(squares,-1.5,1.5,-1.5,1.5)

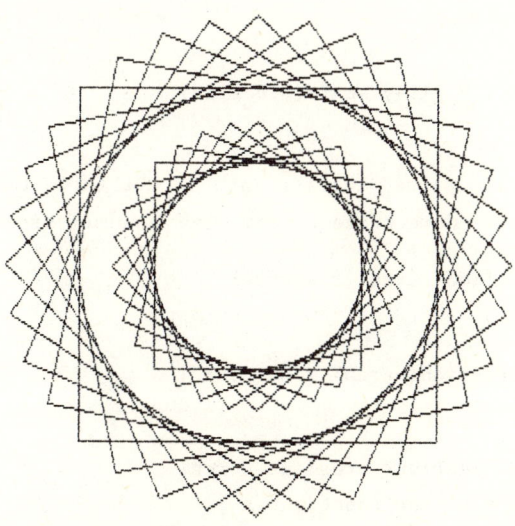

As a second example consider the problem of drawing the two curves

    y1 = a * sin(t + theta)
    y2 = b * cos(t + phi)

and the combined curve y1 + y2 all on the same screen with t going from 0 to 2 * pi in 64 steps. The combined curve will be drawn dotted to distinguish it from the other two. We will assume that a, b, theta, phi together with no.of.steps and y.scale have already been initialised and will only write the plotting procedures and their calls.

  We need first a general purpose plotting procedure which, given a function f(x) and a boolean with name 'dotted' will draw the curve y = f(x). If 'dotted' has value **true** the curve will be drawn dotted by leaving out every other line segment. This is done easily using the '&' and '^' operators alternately. A procedure to do this is as follows

procedure plot.function((**creal** -> **real**) f ; **cbool** dotted)
begin
  let x := 0.0 ; **let** x.inc = 2 * pi / no.of.steps
  let curve := [0,f(0)]
  for i = 1 **to** no.of.steps **do**
  begin
    x := x + x.inc
    curve := **if** dotted **and** i **rem** 2 = 0 **then** curve & [x,f(x)]
                 else curve ^ [x,f(x)]
  end
  draw(curve,0,2 * pi,-y.scale,y.scale)
end

We only need to write procedures for each of the three functions and then to call the plot procedure three times. The function procedures are

procedure sine.function(**creal** x -> **real**)
a * sin(x + theta)

procedure cosine.function(**creal** x -> **real**)
b * cos(x + phi)

procedure combined.function(**creal** x -> **real**)
sine.function(x) + cosine.function(x)

Assuming that the y scale has been defined suitably by

let y.scale = rabs(a) + rabs(b)

We can now complete the program by writing

plot.function(sine.function,**false**)
plot.function(cosine.function,**false**)
plot.function(combined.function,**true**)

together with

draw([0,0] ^ [1,0] & [0,-1] ^ [0,1],0.1,-1,1)

to put in the axes. Notice that we do not need to use the same coordinate space as for the functions since each draw command is independent of all other draw commands. We are only interested in where the picture is to appear on the screen and not in what is already there.

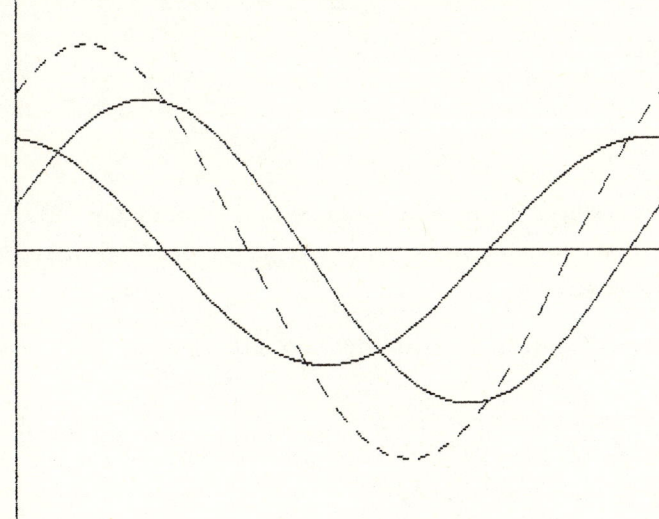

ot of sin and cos with a = 2, b = 1.5, theta = 0.3, phi = 0.1

We conclude this section with a program to draw the Hilbert curve. This is a recursively defined curve which has interesting mathematical properties. The basic element in the general curve is the point origin.

let curve := [0,0]

The definition is recursive taking the figure so far and putting it, suitably rotated, in the four corners of a larger square and joining up the end points to produce the next figure. The first two such operations produce the figures

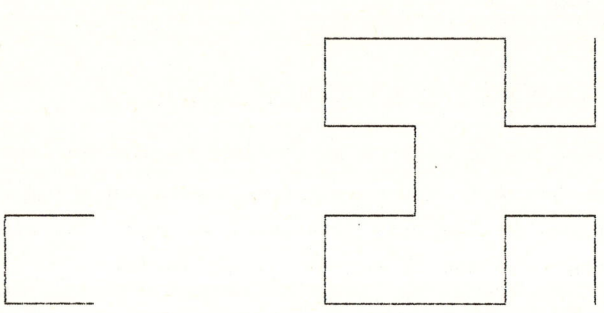

Subsequent figures are obtained by repeating this process on the previous figure. A suitable procedure to produce the next figure from the previous one is

```
procedure Hilbert( cpic p ; creal width -> pic )
begin
    let p1 = rotate p by -90
    let p2 = scale p1 by 1,-1
    let p3 = scale p1 by -1,1
    shift p3 by width + 1,width + 1 ^
    shift p by 0,width + 1 ^
    p ^
    shift p2 by width * 2 + 1,width
end
```

Check to see where each sub-picture goes and its orientation. The rest of the program consists of building up the picture to the required complexity and finally drawing the complete abstract picture.

```
write "Enter degree of complexity, integer range 1 -> 8 >"
let complexity = readi ; let width := 0 ; let curve := [ 0,0 ]
for i = 1 to complexity do
begin
      curve := Hilbert( curve,width )
      width := 2 * width + 1
end
erase.to( "black" )
draw( curve,0,width,0,width )
```

Although the curve is defined recursively the solution here is iterative. This is one of the cases when an iterative solution can be written as clearly as a recursive one. The reader may care to write the solution recursively as an extra exercise.

Exercises 14

14.1 Modify the curve drawing procedure plot.function to include parameters to specify the x and y axis limits and also the number of intervals to be used in the x direction.

14.2 Modify the rotating squares program to draw the picture in each corner of the screen. You will need to use the split.screen function.

14.3 Write a program to read in the coordinates of two points and a piece of text and to write the text on the screen between two points. You will also need to specify the total plot dimensions for the screen.

14.4 Using the separate compilation facility of the S-algol compiler you can build up a library of functions which produce pictures as their result. Write a function to produce a unit circle at the origin. Note that such a function may then be used to define ellipses and circles of any shape, size and orientation.

Solutions to Exercises 14

14.1 The procedure heading needs to be changed to

procedure plot.function(**creal** xmin,xmax,ymin,ymax ; **cint** no.of.steps
                              (**creal** -> **real**) f ; **cbool** dotted)

The other changes are minor and involve the limits for function evaluation and plotting and the calculation of x.inc. The procedure body becomes

begin
    let x := xmin ; **let** x.inc = (xmax - xmin) / no.of.steps
    let curve := [xmin,f(xmin)]
    for i = 1 **to** no.of.steps **do**
    begin
        x := xmin + i * x.inc
        curve := **if** dotted **and** i **rem** 2 = 0 **then** curve.& [x,f(n)]
                                               else curve ^ [x,f(n)]
    end
    draw(curve,xmin,xmax,ymin,ymax)
end

14.2 Only the part of the program to draw the pictures needs to be changed. To split the screen four times can be done in a double **for** loop as follows by four repeated calls of split.screen and draw.

let scrn.div.x = (scrn.x.min + scrn.x.max) **div** 2
let scrn.div.y = (scrn.y.min + scrn.y.max) **div** 2
let scrn.centre.x = scrn.div.x + 1
let scrn.centre.y = scrn.div.y + 1
for i = scrn.x.min **to** scrn.x.min + scrn.centre.x **by** scrn.centre.x **do**

```
    for j = scrn.y.min to scrn.y.min + scrn.centre.y by scrn.centre.y do
    begin
        split.screen( i,i + scrn.div.x,j,j + scrn.div.y )
        draw( squares,-1.5,1.5,-1.5,1.5 )
        draw( squares,-2.6,2.6,-2.6,2.6 )
    end
```

14.3
```
write "Enter string to be plotted 'n"
let s = read.a.line
write "Enter two pairs of coordinates for end points of the string 'n"
let a = readr ; let b = readr
let c = readr ; let d = readr
write "Enter screen limits xmin,xmax,ymin,ymax 'n"
let xmin = readr ; let xmax = readr
let ymin = readr ; let ymax = readr
draw( text s from a,b to c,d,xmin,xmax,ymin,ymax )
?
```

14.4
```
procedure circle( -> pic )
begin
    let theta := 0.0 ; let step := 0.1
    let circle := [ 1,0 ]
    while theta ≤ 2 * pi do
    begin
        theta := theta + step
        circle := circle ^ [ cos( theta ),sin( theta ) ]
    end
    circle
end
```

You can improve on this solution somewhat in the same way the rotating squares program was improved.

```
procedure circle( -> pic )
begin
    let angle = 360 / no.of.sectors ; let half.angle = angle / 2
    let circle := rotate [ 1,1 ] by -half.angle ^
```

```
                    rotate [ 1,1 ] by half.angle
    let i := 1
    while i < no.of.sectors do
    begin
        circle := circle & rotate circle by i * angle
        i := i + i
    end
    circle
end
```

A general ellipse can then be programmed by

```
procedure ellipse( creal x.centre,y.centre,x.scale,y.scale -> pic )
shift scale circle by x.scale,y.scale by x.centre,y.centre
```

15 S-algol DESIGN PHILOSOPHY

In the next two chapters we will take a more formal look at the S-algol language. In this one we will discuss how the language was designed. It is important that the user understands the design philosophy as it gives an insight into the limitations of the language and an indication of its applicability. The user will thus avoid falling into the trap of using S-algol when another software tool is more appropriate.

Programming language design is probably the most emotive subject in Computational Science today. Nearly everyone uses a programming language and most people have something to say about their design. The situation is analogous to mathematics where notations are constantly being invented and improved. There has never been one universal mathematical notation or computer language which suits all tastes and needs, and it is unreasonable to expect that there ever will be. That does not mean that development of further languages is useless. Indeed better languages must be developed continuously in order to achieve greater clarity and levels of abstraction. We hope this development can be done in a disciplined manner.

The languages that we are interested in as a group for development can generally be described as the algols. That is to say, low level languages such as assemblers and machine orientated languages such as PL360 Wirth (1966) will not be discussed. Furthermore, the applicative languages such as the proposed ISWIM family Landin (1966), LISP McCarthy et al (1962) and the more modern sugarings of the lambda calculus like SASL Turner (1979) are also not considered. The discussion is restricted to the algols which can be roughly classified by the following rules.

Scope rules and block structure
Names may be introduced to define local quantities. The names are

undefined outside the local environment. However, different environments may use the same name unambiguously to represent different objects.

Abstraction facility

The algols all have a powerful abstraction mechanism to allow the user to shorten and clarify programs. This is usually in the form of a procedure with parameters.

Compile time type checking

The types of all the expressions in the language can be checked by a static analysis of the program.

Infinite store

The programmer is relieved of the burden of storage allocation and is presented with an infinite capacity to create data objects.

Selective store updating

In conjunction with the infinite store concept, the user is allowed to selectively alter the store. This is usually implemented as an efficiency consideration on present day machines and generally takes the form of an assignment statement. It should be pointed out that it is really this rule that gives rise to the concept of the store.

As with any rough classification, some languages cut across the rules. How well a language fits the rules determines how much of an algol it is. Languages that could be considered as algols are Algol 60 Naur et al (1963), Algol W Wirth & Hoare (1966), Algol S Turner & Morrison (1975), and perhaps Pascal Wirth (1971) and Algol 68 van Wijngaarden et al. (1969).

Where have they gone wrong? Have they? Many criticisms of these languages have appeared, particularly for the more popular ones such as Pascal and Algol 68. They take the form of criticising particular aspects of the languages Dijkstra (1968), Habbermann (1973) and Lecarme & Desjardins (1975) or the overall design Tennent (1977).

It is not part of this work to perform a character assassination on each programming language but merely to report that something is wrong with them. A clue to this malaise is given by Dijkstra (1972)

"Another lesson we should have learned from the recent past is that development of 'richer' or 'more powerful' programming languages was a mistake in the sense that these baroque monstrosities, these conglomerations of idiosyncrasies, are really unmanageable both mechanically and mentally."

Dijkstra points out that our language design has somehow gone wrong in producing languages that we cannot handle intellectually. This leads the programmer to concentrate on the vagaries of the programming language and distracts him from the complexity of the problem.

How then should programming languages be designed? A. van Wijngaarden (1963) with his notion of a generalised algol may be used as a starting point.

"In order that a language be powerful and elegant it should not contain many concepts."

This approach has only one design aim. That aim is an economy of concept where the language will have a small number of general rules with no features or special cases since every exception to a general rule causes the language to become more complex. Occam's Razor is applied wherever possible to preserve the language simplicity. This leads the language designer to formulate the fundamental concepts behind the language and to generalise these ideas wherever possible. Furthermore, the simplicity is not achieved at the expense of power, indeed more power is derived from the lack of restriction. Therefore, simpler but more powerful languages may be designed.

Three general rules to be used as a basis for this type of language design are now proposed.

The Principle of correspondence

This first rule is based on work done by Strachey (1966) and is more clearly reviewed by Tennent (1977). However, the problem was first stated by Landin (1966).

"In almost every language a user can coin names, obeying certain rules about the contexts in which the name is used and their relation to the textual segments that introduce, define, declare or otherwise constrain its use. These rules vary considerably from one language to another, and frequently even within a single language there may be different conventions for different classes of names with near analogies that come irritatingly close to being exact."

Landin points out that all the rules governing names in a language should be designed together in order to avoid irregularities in the manner in which the names may be used. For example, the scope rules should be the same everywhere. In most algols names may only be introduced in declarations and as procedure parameters. Therefore for each type of declaration in the language there should be a corresponding parametric declaration. Indeed parameters should be regarded as locally defined objects. The principle of correspondence goes a little further by taking account of all possible parameter passing modes.

This rule obeys the simplicity yardstick and Tennent performs a comparison on Pascal parametric and declarative objects. Pascal is found to be lacking under this type of analysis since most of the declarative constructs have no parametric equivalent. Most notable is the fact that types may be declared but not passed as parameters thereby disallowing the possibility of abstract data types Liskov et al (1977).

The principle of abstraction

This rule has the same sources as the previous one. Abstraction is a process of extracting the general structure to allow the inessential details to be ignored. This facility is well known to mathematicians and programmers since it is the only tool they have for handling complexity.

The technique when applied to language design is to define all the semantically meaningful syntactic categories in the language and allow an abstraction over them. The most familiar form of abstraction is the function which is an abstraction over expressions. The principle of abstraction is more difficult to apply than the principle of correspondence since it is more difficult to identify the semantically meaningful constructs than it is to identify declarations. Also it is sometimes difficult to visualise the use of an abstraction once it is made.

The principle of data type completeness

This principle, while not explicitly stated by Strachey, is one of which he was well aware. The rule states that all data types must have the same 'civil rights' in the language and that rules for using data types should be complete with no gaps. This means that any general operation such as assignment or passing the data object as a parameter has an equivalent form for all data types.

Examples of lack of completeness can be seen in Algol W where arrays are not allowed as fields of records and in Pascal where only some objects are allowed as elements of sets. This principle will lead to simplicity since it avoids the complexity of special cases.

The conceptual store

Another aspect which will affect the semantic model of the language is that of the conceptual store. It is useful to look at how the store arose as it will give a clearer understanding of why it is there.

In general, mathematics has no concept of a store. There are only expressions which are characterised by having a value. The most useful property of only having a world of expressions is that of **referential transparency** described by Quine (1963). This states that in order to evaluate an expression with sub-expressions all we require to know about the sub-expressions is their values. Anything else, such as the order of evaluation is irrelevant. The applicative languages make use of general mathematical notation and have no underlying concept of a store. Donahue (1977) emphasises that the semantic model for these types of languages is much simpler and Hoare (1975) has proposed a model for data structures in such an environment.

How then does the concept of the store arise? Of course, it comes from the design of computer hardware with high speed stores. To allow the power of these machines to be fully utilised it is necessary to make as best use of the high speed store as possible. It is therefore an efficiency consideration.

The assignment statement is introduced to allow the store to be reused. There are two places where this will improve the efficiency of a program. Firstly in loop control to alter the controlling value and secondly in pointers to allow selective updating of data structures. Since the store may be altered during the dynamic evaluation of the program it also introduces the concept of sequencing and thus commands or statements in the algol sense. Quite often in our programming languages the statement is the basic unit of expression. However, statements can be regarded as mere syntactic sugarings to help us write down more complex expressions. Indeed it is helpful to view the statement as an expression with a void value. It would be useful if the language encouraged this in some manner.

The design approach

Having discussed a number of rules for language design we may now consider how they are used in the design process.

Data types

It is necessary to decide which data types, both simple and compound, are required by the language and to define the operations on these data types. The flavour of the language will be determined by the data objects it can manipulate. The principle of data type completeness is invoked to ensure that all data objects have the same civil rights. Ignoring the principle means introducing rules to handle exceptions thus making the language more complex. For example, if arrays are allowed then arrays of arrays should be allowed as should expressions and functions with array results.

The store

The store, if any, and the manner in which it may be used must be decided. First of all the relationship between the store and the data types should be defined. This includes the implementation of pointers, data locations and protection on these locations. For example, constants may be regarded as storage locations which may not be updated Gunn & Morrison (1979).

The introduction of the store forces consideration of the language control structures. An excellent paper by Ledgard & Marcotty (1975) addresses itself to this subject.

Abstraction

Tennent (1977) has suggested that the method of applying the principle of abstraction is to identify the semantically meaningful syntactic categories and invent abstractions for each. This he does for Pascal and proposes some extensions to complete the abstractions. However, he points out that it is not always an easy matter to identify these categories in the first place. Most languages have at least the following.

Syntactic category	Abstraction
expression	function
statement	procedure
declaration	module

sequencer   sequel

Functions and procedures should be familiar. The name module derives from Schuman (1974) and the sequel from Tennent.

The problem is to identify the useful abstractions. For example, for those of us in love with the algol scope rules, the module is a peculiar abstraction especially since the same power can be derived from function producing functions.

Declarations and parameters

Declarations and parametric objects must be considered together. There must be a one to one correspondence between the two. This does not mean that they necessarily have the same syntax but that for every type of declaration there is an equivalent parametric type. Parameter passing modes are also included in this correspondence. For example, the declarative equivalent of call by value is an initialising declaration. If functions, record classes etc. can be declared then they can be passed as parameters. Finally, if the language has a facility to define new data types and give them a name then the type can be passed as a parameter rather like extended Algol 68 modals Lindsay (1974).

Input and output

The I/O models for most high level languages tend to reflect the environment in which they were designed. Some attempts have been made to design and implement comprehensive I/O systems. Unfortunately where it has not been tied to particular hardware it has never been very successful. Nowhere else in the design of a programming language does the hardware intervene as much as it does in the I/O system. When a new I/O device becomes available the language must be able to make use of it. Of course, this situation is hopeless and perhaps the wisest approach to I/O is to allow the implementor to deal with it for a particular environment, as the Algol 60 designers proposed.

Iterate

Re-evaluate the language and correct or justify any idiosyncrasies in the design. Hopefully the design process will converge.

Concrete syntax

The final stage of language design is to propose a concrete syntax. Ideally different groups of workers could have a different syntax if desired. However, there are many users who do not wish to design their own syntax and so the language must provide at least one possibility.

It seems very obvious to say that the syntax should be simple and easy to learn. That may be so but there is no doubt that some of the success of the language depends on the cosmetics. Also, a carefully chosen syntax can ease the problem of compilation. Wirth (1974) has this to say.

"Adhere to a syntactic structure that can be analysed by a simple technique such as recursive descent with one symbol look-ahead. This not only aids the compiler, but also the programmer, and is vital for the successful diagnosis of errors."

The design of the syntax is also a balance between brevity and clarity. An example of this design tension is illustrated by the different rules for introducing names in S-algol and is discussed later.

S-algol design

The S-algol language is designed on the principles outlined above. A discussion of the main concepts of the language is now given. As with most other languages there is a tension between the design aims and a practical implementation. Whenever one of the principles has been violated a complete discussion of the issues involved is given. However, in the main, adherence to the three tenets has led to a very simple language based on the fact that there are fewer rules and exceptions.

The description of the main issues in the language follows the method of development. However, since the language exists, it has a concrete syntax for at least one implementation. Where it is felt necessary this concrete syntax has been used for clarity in the description.

The discussion begins with the design of the data types.

The universe of discourse

The data types in S-algol are defined by the following rules.

(a) The scalar data types are integer, real, boolean, file and string. Little requires to be said about the types integer, real and boolean since most programmers are aware of them and S-algol has the usual range of operations on these types. The type file is an I/O stream to which or from which data objects may be placed or taken respectively. Finally, type string represents the set of all possible collections of characters in the character set. At first this seems to be a compound data object and is regarded as such by some. However, it is unnecessarily complex to introduce a type char and a compound type string for all types. The concept is too close to a vector for comfort and is further confused by the difference between vectors of characters and strings of characters. By including strings and not characters as a scalar data type this confusion is avoided and a simple method of allowing the basic operations on strings is available. These operations are concatenation, substring selection, length and all the relational operations. This approach is much more pleasant than having, as in Pascal, arrays of characters.

(b) For any data type T, *T is the data type of a vector with components of type T. Note that the bounds of the vector are not part of its type and are determined dynamically. Multi-dimensional arrays can be implemented as vectors of vectors.

(c) The data type structure comprises of any number of fields and any data type in each field. Each user defined structure class has a fixed number of fields of fixed type. The class of a structure, like the bounds of a vector is not part of the type but is again determined dynamically.

To ensure the principle of data type completeness is followed the world of data objects is given as the closure of rule (a) under the recursive application of rules (b) and (c). This, of course, gives an infinite number of data types. Anywhere in the language where a data type is referred to, care must be taken to ensure that all data types are acceptable. In this manner all data types will have the same civil rights. This need not be the case for infix operators as these are merely syntactic sugarings of commonly used functions and have no bearing on the semantic model.

The S-algol conceptual store

The store concept, in the algols, arises from the practicality of efficient implementations of programs on von Neumann machines. As mentioned above one of the areas in which efficiency will be improved is in the implementation of large data structures. In S-algol, the vectors and structures have full civil rights and may be assigned. From an efficiency point of view it is unwise to copy these objects on assignment and a slightly different view of vectors and structures must be taken for an efficient implementation.

Objects of type *T and pntr are regarded as pointers to vectors and structures respectively. The value of a vector or a structure is defined as the pointer. Therefore on assignment or similar operations only the pointer is copied.

The definition of equality on all data types can now be regarded as a comparison of their values. However, it must always be remembered that the value of a compound data object is the pointer.

Furthermore, the problem of the general pointer or L-value as Strachey would call it has been raised. Let us quickly kill it by using as evidence against, the objections raised by Hoare (1975) and the disastrous effects it has had on Algol 68 such as the dangling reference. It is bad enough having a restricted pointer for efficiency's sake.

The semantic model of the store is one with L-values and R-values for each data type. That is, the values in all data types may be assigned to a location. In general L-values cannot be passed around only assigned to. However, vectors and structures contain L-values which themselves contain the R-values of the elements.

One further concept to be discussed in relation to the store is protection and in particular constancy.

The concept of a variable is one which is well established in the current algols. It takes the form of a name which may alter its value during the execution of the program. The variable is implemented by a location which contains its value. When a variable is updated its R-value is altered. Constants, by comparison, are not often found as a separate concept, although the majority of variables would be better implemented as constants since they never alter their value. A constant is an object whose value is invariant. It may be initialised but never altered in its lifetime. Like a variable, a constant has an L-value and an R-value, but any attempt to update it will produce an error. According to Strachey (1967)

"Constancy is an attribute of the L-value, and is moreover an invariant property. Thus when we create a new L-value, ..., we must decide whether it is variable or constant."

The manifest constants of BCPL Richards (1969) and Pascal do not meet this definition of constancy. They are compile time objects and

are not implemented as protected locations. Furthermore, the issue of
constancy extends beyond the world of scalar data objects. As the
definition points out, anywhere an L-value is introduced it must have the
option of being constant or variable. Therefore, in addition to the scalar
values being constant so also may structures, their fields, vectors and
their elements be constant. A fuller discussion on the concept of
constancy is given by Gunn & Morrison (1979).

Control structures

The introduction of the store forces consideration of the
language control structures. Ledgard & Marcotty (1975) have classified
control structures and S-algol falls into their D′ category. Their
conclusion is that the correct balance between power and security is given
by this category. S-algol is an expression orientated language and it
regards a statement as an expression of type void. The selection clauses
are **if** ..... **then** ..... **else** which degenerates to **if** ..... **do** for the
single pronged version, and a **case** clause. The **case** clause is a new type
of case statement where the case selector is of any type and is matched
with expressions of the same type to find the selected clause. The
matching test is the equality test and the tests are performed in order so
that the programmer can place the most likely one first. This is rather
like the guarded commands of Dijkstra (1975) with the non-determinism
removed.

The rest of the control structures are fairly conventional.
They are **while** ... **do** , **repeat** ... **while** and **repeat** ... **while** ... **do** which
give loops with tests at the start, end and middle of loops. The **for** loop
is similar to that proposed by Hoare (1972). The control identifier is
constant and is redefined every time round the loop. The initial value,
step and limit are restricted to integers and evaluated only once.

Abstractions

A table is given for S-algol

Syntactic category	Abstraction
typed clause	typed procedure
untyped clause	untyped procedure
declaration	module
sequencer	sequel

Procedures are familiar, the abstractions over declarations and sequencers are not. Tennent use the name module after Schuman for a declaration abstraction. The problem with this is that it destroys the block structured scope rules of algol. His abstraction over sequencers is a sequel which is just another convoluted goto. Ledgard and Marcotty are extremely critical of this type of branch. On the other hand Knuth (1974) defends it.

The problem now is to identify the useful abstractions. The procedure is an old and trusted friend. The sequel looks dangerous and confusing. The module at first glance looks useful but it destroys the scope rules. In the final analysis S-algol rejected the module and the sequel. It is interesting to note that the language has only four semantically meaningful syntactic categories which perhaps highlights its simplicity.

Declarations and parameters

In the modern algols a plethora of parameter passing modes has evolved. It is usually one of the most difficult areas to understand in a language and is certainly complex to teach. By considering the declarative and parametric mechanisms together and applying the principle of correspondence, it is hoped that a simpler and more elegant solution will be found.

Declaring a name and giving a value or calling a procedure sets up a correspondence between the formal parameter (name) and the actual parameter (value). When a data object is declared in S-algol it must be given an initial value. This avoids one type of programming error completely and corresponds to **call by value** for parameters. Assignment to a formal parameter inside a procedure has no effect outside and the value will disappear on exit. With both declarations and parameters an L-value has been introduced and the syntax must allow for it being constant or variable. This does not effect the parameter passing mode it merely determines whether assignments to the location are allowed. Thus S-algol has only **call by value** with the procedure being able to return a value which may be scalar or compound.

Names may also be introduced to represent a structure class or a procedure. To complete the principle of correspondence there must be a parametric equivalent. In order to preserve the strong typing in the language, a procedure passed as a parameter must specify its parameter types and the same is true for a structure class. The table below gives the S-algol declarative and parametric correspondence.

Denotation	Declarative construct	Parametric Construct	
		Formal	Actual
Initialised name with constant value	let I = E, for I = E....	cT I	E
Initialised name with variable value	let I := E	T I	E
structure	structure I(t1I1,....tnIn)	same	I
procedure	procedure I(t1I1,....tnIn)	(t1,...tn)I	I

The input output model

The S-algol solution is to propose an I/O model but to invite the implementor to alter the model in the spirit of the language whenever it is considered necessary. By designing an extremely simple I/O system it is hoped that together with the abstraction facilities in the language, it will be powerful enough to handle any environment. This is perhaps a forlorn hope.

The S-algol I/O system is based on files which contain a sequence of characters. Files may be created, deleted, and generally manipulated within a program. A file descriptor is a data type with full civil rights. The file system has functions which act on files to perform the I/O. **read** and **write** are two of these functions.

This very simple system is extremely powerful especially when combined with the S-algol abstraction facilities but the specific details will necessarily differ from implementation to implementation.

The concrete syntax

The algols have often been criticised for being long-winded. This has generally been due to the restrictive syntax and not the semantic model. Such a syntax is usually there to ease the task of compilation and in particular error recovery. However, it makes the programmer's job more difficult especially if the error recovery is not used. An example of how this long-windedness can be avoided is given in the rules for introducing names in S-algol.

When an object is declared, its name, its value, its type and whether it is a constant or variable is required by the compiler. The problem is how concise can this be made without being obscure. For declarations S-algol has

>**let** I := E

where I is the identifier and E is any valid expression.

e.g.

>**let** a := 2

tells the compiler that a variable 'a' of type integer and initial value 2 has been introduced. The compiler does not need to be told the type, it can deduce it from the expression enabling it to be brief. For constants '=' is used instead of ':='.

e.g.

>**let** a = 13.2 * 2.15

introduces a real constant.

It is possible for the compiler to deduce the types of all the data objects without the program ever having to mention them explicitly. But is it wise?

Take for example a procedure heading. The compiler can deduce from the calls of the procedure, the parameter types and whether they are consistent. However, it cannot deduce whether the formal parameter is constant or variable. Furthermore, the procedure should be understandable without reference to the calls. Therefore it is sensible to force the user to specify the object type and whether or not it is constant. Finally, if the procedure returns a value it is aesthetically pleasing to have the object type specified in the procedure heading. It should be emphasised that this should not be confused with the principle of correspondence as it is merely fitting a convenient syntax around the semantic model.

One particularly annoying feature of most algols is that all declarations must come before statements in a block. In S-algol there is no **goto** clause and therefore the programmer cannot jump round a declaration. By insisting that everything is declared before it is used except in the case of mutually recursive procedures, the rules on the position of a declaration can be relaxed. In S-algol, declarations may be freely mixed with statements. The scope of a name is from immediately after the declaration to the end of the block. This allows names to be introduced as locally as possible. Again it should be noted that this is merely a syntactic extension.

Conclusions

It has been observed that our general purpose programming languages were becoming intellectually unmanageable. It was therefore felt that an attempt to place language design on a firmer basis was necessary.

The method is based around three rules which are well known to workers in the field of semantics. They are

The principle of correspondence
The principle of abstraction
The principle of data type completeness

Hitherto these rules have been used in the analysis of languages to highlight their differences and shortcomings. Here they are used in the synthesis of a programming language with the aim that they simplify and somehow make the language more intellectually manageable. This simplicity is not achieved at the expense of power, indeed more power is derived from the simplicity or rather from the lack of restriction.

The language that is the result of all this careful design is S-algol. In what way is the language new or better? What are the innovations?

First of all, S-algol is not without innovations. In particular, the strings as a scalar data type, only allowing initialising declarations and call by value parameters, the **case** clause, the mixing of clauses and declarations and introducing constancy as a protection issue are all new. Although these ideas help, the strength of the language does not derive from them. It comes from the fact that it is carefully designed from a set of rules that allow few exceptions to the general case. Thus, at least S-algol can be assessed scientifically using these ground rules.

16 S-algol SYNTAX

We are now ready to study a more precise definition of S-algol. It is important that a programming language can be formally defined since it gives implementors a standard to work on. There are two levels of definition, syntactic and semantic. The previous chapters of this book give an informal semantics of S-algol. A more formal semantic description is given by Morrison (1979) and a denotational semantics by Adamson (1982). Here we will deal with the formal syntactic rules. That is we will define the set of all syntactically legal S-algol programs. It should be remembered however that the meaning of any one of these programs is defined by the semantics.

To define the syntax of a language we need another notation which we will call a **meta language** and in this case we choose a variation of the two level grammars of van Wijngaarden (1969).

The syntax of S-algol is specified by a set of rules or **productions** as they are normally called. Each production specifies the manner in which a particular syntactic category (e.g. a clause) can be formed. The syntactic category name is enclosed in the meta symbols '<' and '>' thus distinguishing it from names or reserved words in the language. These syntactic categories can be mixed in productions with terminal symbols which are actual symbols of the language itself. Thus by following the production until we only have terminal symbols we can derive legal programs. We can also use the productions in a compiler to check that a program is legal and a very efficient method of doing this, called Recursive Descent is described by Davie & Morrison (1981). Other meta symbols include '|' which allows a choice in a production. The braces '{' and '}' are used in pairs to enclose anything that is optional and if the syntactic object can appear zero or many times the braces are followed by a '*'. The square brackets '[' and ']' are also used in pairs to denote an object that must occur at least once. When used with a '*' we have a one or many times repetition. You should not confuse the meta symbols '|','<', '>', '*', '[', ']', '{' and '}' with the actual symbols in S-algol and we will be careful to keep the two concepts completely separate in our description.

As you may expect with any reasonable programming language the productions for S-algol are recursive which means that there are an infinite number of legal S-algol programs. However the syntax of S-algol can be described in about 60 productions. We will break ourselves in gently with an example.

<identifier> ::= <letter>{<letter>|<digit>|.}*

indicates that an identifier can be formed as a letter followed by zero or many letters, digits or dots.

It is not always as easy as the above example. For example we sometimes have to restrict the possibilities of a production by specifying the legal types for the production. e.g.

<literal> ::= <int-literal>|<real-literal>|<bool-literal>|
<string-literal>|<file-literal>|<pntr-literal>

denotes that a literal can be any one of the types indicated but cannot be for example a vector literal since no such object exists in S-algol. Notice that we have placed the type name inside the angled brackets but separated it from the syntactic category name by a '-'. We will see that we can also have generic type categories which we will write in capital letters but before that we must look at the S-algol type structure.

There are an infinite number of data types in S-algol defined recursively by the following rules.

(a) The scalar data types are int, real, bool, string and file.
(b) For any data type T, *T is the data type of a vector with elements of type T.
(c) The data type pntr comprises a structure with any number of fields, and any data type in each field.

In addition to the above data types there are a number of other objects in S-algol to which it is convenient to give a type in order that the compiler may check their use for consistency.

(d) The type of a procedure with parameters T1,......,Tn and result type Tm is (T1,......,Tn -> Tm).

(e) Clauses which yield no value are of type void.

(f) The class of a structure with fields of type T1,....Tn is of type (T1,.....,Tn)-structure and its fields are of type Ti-field.

The user requires to know about these types in order to follow the complete type matching rules. From the above types we can describe the generic types that we require for the formal definition of S-algol. They are

```
T0 ::= int|real
T1 ::= T0|string
T2 ::= T1|bool
T3 ::= T2|pntr|file
T4 ::= T3|*T4
T5 ::= T4|void
T6 ::= T5|structure|T4.field|T5.procedure
```

These are rules about our meta rules and are sometimes called **hyper rules**. It is not obvious how these generic types come about. Indeed they are defined with hindsight of what is required in the language and we should remember that they are being used in a description of the language. We can easily identify some of these generic types. For example, T0 is the arithmetic types and T4 is all the data types including vectors.

The full syntax of S-algol is given in Appendix I. We will go through a little of the definition here highlighting points as it is felt necessary.

The form of a complete S-algol program is

<void-program> ::= <void-sequence>?

That is a valid program must be of type void and it can only be made up by a sequence of type void followed by a '?'. Sequences can be

<T5-sequence> ::= [<declaration>|<void-clause>];<T5-sequence>|
        <T5-clause>
<void-sequence> ::= <declaration>

A declaration is always of type void. However a sequence can be any of the T5 types and is made up of any number of declarations or clauses in any order but separated by semi-colons. The type of the sequence is the type of the last clause in the sequence and if there is more than one clause all but the last must be void.

There are several types of clauses defined by

```
<void-clause> ::= if<bool-clause>do<void-clause>|
                  repeat<void-clause>while<bool-clause>{do<void-clause>}|
                  while<bool-clause>do<void-clause>|
                  for<int-identifier>=<int-clause>to<int-clause>
                     {by<int-clause>}do<void-clause>|
                  <write>|
                  <T4-assign>:=<T4-clause>|
                  <void-expression>

<T5-clause>  ::= if<bool-clause>then<T5-clause>else<T5-clause>|
                 case<T4-clause>of
                 [<T4-clause>{,T4-clause>}*:<T5-clause>;]*
                    default:<T5-clause>|
                 <T4-expression>
```

All these clauses have been described earlier in this book and need not be repeated here. We are, however, concerned with all the legal possibilities in forming programs and it is worth emphasising the following points. The single armed version of the **if** clause is void whereas the double version can be any of the T5 types. The boolean clauses of the **if** and **while** clauses allow for arbitrary complexity. The initialisation, step and limit in the **for** clause are all integers and the selector type in the **case** clause can be any one of T4 but the result can be any one of T5. In all the productions the substitution of one type for a generic type must be done consistently. For example, if one part of the **case** clause is of type void in the substitution for T5 then so must all the rest. Anything else is illegal. Finally only objects with type T4 can be assigned to and as we will see later the definition includes vector elements and structure fields.

The syntax of expressions is given in such a manner as to preserve the precedence table for operators given in Chapter 8. Boolean expressions can be formed by

```
<bool-expression> ::= <bool-exp0>{or<bool-exp0>}*
<bool-exp0>      ::= <bool-exp1>{and<bool-exp1>}*
<bool-exp1>      ::= <T1-exp3> [<ang>|≤|≥|<gle>]<T1-exp3> |
                     <T4-exp2> [=|≠]<T4-exp2> |
                     <pntr-exp3> [is|isnt]<structure-identifier>
<bool-exp2>      ::= {~}<bool-exp3>
```

Both **and** and **or** which can be freely mixed in boolean expressions are non-strict. That is the left to right evaluation of a boolean expression stops as soon as the result is known. For example

    true or <exp>

gives the value true without executing the code for <exp>. Note also that '~' has a higher priority than all the other relational operators and that equality '=' is defined on all the S-algol data types.

The rest of the syntactic description of S-algol is now pretty straightforward and contains all the details of the language even down to how to form names and literals. Perhaps the most subtle point of the language is how clauses may be used in expressions if surrounded by brackets and how sequences can become expressions and clauses in certain circumstances when enclosed by **begin end**. We will say no more about the S-algol syntax here but invite you to spend some time unravelling the secrets of the description in Appendix I.

REFERENCES

Adamson, I.A.T. (1982). The denotational semantics of S-algol. M.Sc. Thesis University of St Andrews.
Ball, W.W.R. (1896). Mathematical Recreations and Problems. Macmillan.
Cole, A.J. & Morrison, R. (1980). Linguistic Disfigurement. Computing Vol 8.
Cole, A.J. (1981). Macro Processors. Cambridge University Press.
Cole, A.J. & Morrison, R. (1982). Triplex : a system for interval arithmetic. Software, Practice & Experience Vol 12,4
Davie, A.J.T. & Morrison, R. (1981). Recursive Descent Compiling. Ellis-Horwood Press.
Dijkstra, E.W. (1968). Goto statement considered harmful. Comm.ACM 11,3 147-8
Dijkstra, E.W. (1972). The humble programmer. Comm.ACM 15,18 859-866.
Dijkstra, E.W. (1975). Guarded commands, nondeterminacy and formal derivation. CACM Vol 18 No 8.
Donahue, J.E. (1977). Locations considered unnecessary. Acta Informatica 8 221-242.
Gunn, H.I.E. & Morrison, R. (1979). On the implementation of constants. Information Processing Letters 9,1 1-4.
Habbermann, A.N. (1973). Critical comments on the programming language Pascal. Acta Informatica 3 47-57.
Hoare, C.A.R. (1972). A note on the for statement. BIT Vol 12 334-341.
Hoare, C.A.R. (1975). Recursive data structures. Int. J. of Computer and System Sciences Vol 4 105-132.
Knuth, D.E. (1974). Structured programming with goto statements. Computing Surveys Vol 6 261-301.
Landin, P.J. (1966). The next 700 programming languages. Comm.ACM 9,3 157-164.
Lecarme, O. & Desjardins, P. (1975). More comments on the programming language Pascal. Acta Informatica 4 231-243.
Ledgard, H.F. & Marcotty, M. (1975). A genealogy of control structures. Comm.ACM 18,11 629-639.

Lindsay, C.H. (1974). Modals. Algol Bulletin 37.4.3.
Liskov, B.H. et al (1977). Abstraction mechanisms in CLU. Comm.ACM 20,8 564-576.
McCarthy, J. et al (1962). Lisp 1.5 Programmers manual. M.I.T. Press Cambridge Mass.
Morrison, R. (1979). S-algol language reference manual. University of St Andrews CS/79/1.
Morrison, R. (1982a). S-algol : a simple algol. Computer Bulletin II/31.
Morrison, R. (1982b). The string as a simple data type. Sigplan Notices Vol 17,3.
Morrison, R. (1982c). Outline Graphics. University of St Andrews. CS/82/2.
Naur, P. et al (1963). Revised report on the algorithmic language Algol 60. Comm.ACM 6,1 1-17.
Quine, W.O. (1963). Set theory and its logic. Harvard University Press.
Richards, M. (1969). BCPL, a tool for compiler writing and systems programming. AFIPS SJCC.
Schuman, S.A. (1974). Towards modular programming in high level languages. Algol Bulletin 37 12-23 .
Strachey, C. (1966). Towards a formal semantics. Formal language description languages, North-Holland .
Strachey, C. (1967). Fundamental concepts in programming languages. Oxford University Press.
Tennent, R.D. (1977). Language design methods based on semantic principles. Acta Informatica 8 97-112.
Turner, D.A. & Morrison, R. (1975). Towards portable compilers. University of St Andrews. TR/75/5.
Turner, D.A. (1979). SASL language manual. University of St Andrews CS/79/3.
van Wijngaarden, A. (1963). Generalised algol. Annual Review of automatic programming 3 17-26.
van Wijngaarden, A. et al (1969). Report on the algorithmic language Algol 68. Numerische Mathematik 14 79-218.
Wirth, N. (1966). PL360 A programming language for the 360 computer. JACM Vol 15 P 36.
Wirth, N. & Hoare, C.A.R. (1966). A contribution to the development of algol. Comm.ACM 9,6 413-431.
Wirth, N. (1971). The programming language Pascal. Acta Informatica 1 35-63.
Wirth, N. (1974). On the design of programming languages. IFIP Congress, North-Holland 386-393.

APPENDIX I

S-algol syntax

Hyper rules

```
T0 ::= int|real
T1 ::= T0|string
T2 ::= T1|bool
T3 ::= T2|pntr|file
T4 ::= T3|*T4
T5 ::= T4|void
T6 ::= T5|structure|T4.field|T5.procedure
```

Meta rules

```
<void-program> ::= <void-sequence>?

<T5-sequence> ::= [<declaration>|<void-clause>];<T5-sequence>|
                  <T5-clause>
<void-sequence> ::= <declaration>

<void-clause> ::= if<bool-clause>do<void-clause>|
                  repeat<void-clause>while<bool-clause>{do<void-clause>}|
                  while<bool-clause>do<void-clause>|
                  for<int-identifier>=<int-clause>to<int-clause>
                     {by<int-clause>}do<void-clause>|
                  <write>|
                  <T4-assign>:=<T4-clause>|
                  <void-expression>

<T5-clause> ::= if<bool-clause>then<T5-clause>else<T5-clause>|
                case<T4-clause>of
                [<T4-clause>{,T4-clause>}*:<T5-clause>;]*
```

```
                    default:<T5-clause>|
                <T4-expression>

<write>       ::= write<write.list>|
                output<file-clause>,<write.list>|
                out.byte<file-clause>,<int-clause>,<int-clause>
<write.list> ::= <T2-clause>{:<int-clause>}{,<write.list>}

<T5-expression> ::= <T5-exp3>
<bool-expression> ::= <bool-exp0>{or<bool-exp0>}*
<bool-exp0>  ::= <bool-exp1>{and<bool-exp1>}*
<bool-exp1>  ::= <T1-exp3>[<ang>|<|<gle>|>]<T1-exp3>|
                <T4-exp2>[=|≠]<T4-exp2>|
                <pntr-exp3>[is|isnt]<structure-identifier>
<bool-exp2>  ::= {~}<bool-exp3>
<T5-exp2>    ::= <T5-exp3>
<T5-exp3>    ::= <T5-exp4>
<T0-exp3>    ::= <T0-exp4>[[+|-]<T0-exp4>]*
<T5-exp4>    ::= <T5-exp5>
<real-exp4>  ::= <real-exp5>[[<star>|/]<real-exp5>]*
<int-exp4>   ::= <int-exp5>[[<star>|div|rem]<int-exp5>]*
<T5-exp5>    ::= <T5-exp6>
<T0-exp5>    ::= [+|-]<T0-exp6>
<T5-exp6>    ::= <T5-exp7>
<string-exp6> ::= <string-exp7>[++<string-exp7>]*
<T5-exp7>    ::= <T5-name>|
                <cur><T5-sequence><ly>|
                begin<T5-sequence>end
<T4-exp7>    ::= (<T4-clause>)
<T3-exp7>    ::= <T3-literal>

<string-exp7> ::= <string-expression>[(<int-clause><bar><int-clause>)]*

<*T4-exp7>   ::= @<int-clause>of<T4-type1><bra><T4-clause.list><ket>|
                vector<bounds>of<T4-clause>
<bounds>     ::= <int-clause>::<int-clause>{,<bounds>}


<T4-assign>  ::= <T4-identifier>|<T4-vec.exp>|<T4-struct.exp>
<T4-vec.exp> ::= <*T4-expression>[(<int-clause.list>)]*
```

```
<T4-struct.exp>       ::= <pntr-expression>[(<T4.field-identifier.list>)]*
<T4-clause.list>      ::= <T4-clause>{,<T4-clause.list>}

<pntr-name>           ::= <pntr-structure.creation>
<T4-name>             ::= <T4-identifier>|<T4-vec.exp>|<T4-struct.exp>
<T5-name>             ::= <T5-proc.call>|<T5-standard.name>
<T5-proc.call>        ::= <T5.procedure-identifier>{(<args.list>)}
<args.list>           ::= [<T4-clause>|<T5.procedure-identifier>|
                          <structure-identifier>]{,<args.list>}
<structure.creation>  ::= <structure-identifier>{(<T4-clause.list>)}
<int-standard.name>   ::= [lwb|upb](<*T4-clause>)|
                          [readi|read.byte]{(<file-clause>)}
<bool-standard.name>  ::= [eof|readb]{(<file-clause>)}
<string-standard.name> ::= [read|peek|reads|read.name|
                          read.a.line]{(<file-clause>)}
<real-standard.name>  ::= readr{(<file-clause>)}
<void-standard.name>  ::= abort

<bool-literal>        ::= true|false
<file-literal>        ::= nullfile
<pntr-literal>        ::= nil
<real-literal>        ::= <int-literal>{.<int-literal>}{e{+|-}<int-literal>}
<int-literal>         ::= [<digit>]*
<string-literal>      ::= "{<char>}*"
<digit>               ::= 0|1|2|3|4|5|6|7|8|9
<char>                ::= any ascii character
<T6-identifier>       ::= <letter>{<letter>|<digit>|.}*
<letter>              ::= A|B|C|D|E|F|G|H|I|J|K|L|M|N|O|P|Q|R|S|T|U|V|W|X|Y|Z|
                          a|b|c|d|e|f|g|h|i|j|k|l|m|n|o|p|q|r|s|t|u|v|w|x|y|z

<declaration>         ::= <let.decl>|<structure.decl>|<procedure.decl>|
                          <external>|<forward>
<let.decl>            ::= let<T4-identifier>[=|:=]<T4-clause>
<structure.decl>      ::= structure<structure-identifier>{(<field.list>)}
<field.list>          ::= <T4-type1><T4.field-identifier.list>{;<field.list>}
<procedure.decl>      ::= procedure<T5.procedure-identifier>
                          {<T5-type.spec>};<T5-clause>
<void-type.spec>      ::= (<param.list>)
<T4-type.spec>        ::= ({<param.list>}<arrow><T4-type>)
```

```
<param.list> ::= <param.spec>{;<param.list>}
<param.spec> ::= <T4-type1><T4-identifier.list>|<structure.decl>|
                 <T5-proc.type><T5.procedure-identifier.list>
<T5-proc.type> ::= ({<arg.type.list>}{<arrow><T4-type>})
<arg.type.list> ::= [<T4-type1>|<T5-proc.type>|
                    <s.type>]{,<arg.type.list>}
<s.type> ::= structure{(<T4-type1>{,<T4-type1>}*)}
<external> ::= external<T5.procedure-identifier>{<T5-proc.type>}
<forward> ::= forward<T5.procedure-identifier>{<T5-proc.type>}
<T6-identifier.list> ::= <T6-identifier>{,<T6-identifier>}*
<T4-type1> ::= {c}<T4-type>
<T4-type> ::= int|real|bool|string|pntr|file|<*T4-type>
<*T4-type> ::= <star><T4-type1>
<arrow> ::= ->
<cur> ::= {
<ly> ::= }
<bra> ::= [
<ket> ::= ]
<star> ::= *
<ang> ::= <
<gle> ::= >
```

APPENDIX II

ASCII codes

0	nul	1	soh	2	stx	3	etx	4	eot	5	enq	6	ack	7	bel
8	bs	9	ht	10	nl	11	vt	12	ff	13	cr	14	so	15	si
16	dle	17	dc1	18	dc2	19	dc3	20	dc4	21	nak	22	syn	23	etb
24	can	25	em	26	sub	27	esc	28	fs	29	gs	30	rs	31	us
32	sp	33	!	34	"	35	#	36	$	37	%	38	&	39	'
40	(	41	)	42	*	43	+	44	,	45	-	46	.	47	/
48	0	49	1	50	2	51	3	52	4	53	5	54	6	55	7
56	8	57	9	58	:	59	;	60	<	61	=	62	>	63	?
64	@	65	A	66	B	67	C	68	D	69	E	70	F	71	G
72	H	73	I	74	J	75	K	76	L	77	M	78	N	79	O
80	P	81	Q	82	R	83	S	84	T	85	U	86	V	87	W
88	X	89	Y	90	Z	91	[	92	\	93	]	94	^	95	_
96	`	97	a	98	b	99	c	100	d	101	e	102	f	103	g
104	h	105	i	106	j	107	k	108	l	109	m	110	n	111	o
112	p	113	q	114	r	115	s	116	t	117	u	118	v	119	w
120	x	121	y	122	z	123	{	124	|	125	}	126	~	127	del

APPENDIX III

List of reserved words

```
if       do       is       or       to       of       by
let      end      int      and      for      rem      div      upb      lwb      eof      nil
then     else     pntr     bool     real     cint     case     isnt     peek
read     file     true
begin    while    cfile    write    creal    cbool    cpntr    readi
readr    readb    reads    abort    false
vector   string   output   repeat
forward  default  cstring
out.byte nullfile
structure   procedure   read.name   read.byte
read.a.line
```

APPENDIX IV

Standard functions

procedure sqrt(**real** x -> **real**)
! the positive square root of x where x ≥ 0

procedure exp(**real** x -> **real**)
! e to the power x

procedure ln(**real** x -> **real**)
! the logarithm of x to the base e where x > 0

procedure sin(**real** x -> **real**)
! sine of x(radians)

procedure cos(**real** x -> **real**)
! cosine of x(radians)

procedure atan(**real** x -> **real**)
! arctangent of x (radians) where - pi / 2 < atan(x) <   pi / 2

procedure code(**int** n -> **string**)
! string of length 1 where s(1|1) = character with
! numeric code abs(n **rem** 128)

procedure decode(**string** s -> **int**)
! numeric code for s(1|1)

procedure truncate(**real** x -> **int**)
! the integer i such that |i| ≤ |x| < |i| + 1 where i * x ≥ 0

procedure line.number(-> **int**)
! the program line number

```
procedure rabs( real x -> real )
! the absolute value of real number x

procedure abs( int n -> int )
! the absolute value of integer n

procedure length( string s -> int )
! the number of characters in the string s

procedure eformat( real n ; int w,d -> string )
! the string representing n with w digits
! before the decimal point and d digits after

procedure fformat( real n ; int w,d -> string )
! the string representing n with w digits
! before the decimal point and d digits after

procedure gformat( real n -> string )
! the string representing n in eformat or
! fformat whichever is suitable

procedure letter( string s -> bool )
! length( s ) = 1 and
! s >= "A" and s <= "Z" or
! s >= "a" and s <= "z"

procedure digit( string s -> bool )
! length( s ) = 1 and
! s >= "0" and s <= "9"

procedure iformat( int n -> string )
! integer n as a string of characters

procedure options( -> *cstring )
! the command line options are given as a vector of strings

procedure shift.l( int value,count -> int )
! shift the first parameter left 'count' places
! bringing in zeros at the low order end

procedure shift.r( int value,count -> int )
! shift the first parameter right 'count' places
! bringing in zeros at the high order end
```

procedure b.and(**int** value1,value2 -> **int**)
! logical 'and' of value1 and value2

procedure b.or(**int** value1,value2 -> **int**)
! logical 'or' of value1 and value2

procedure fiddle.r(**real** n -> ***int**)
! split a real into a vector of two integers.

CPM only

procedure iport(**int** port.number -> **int**)
! read the next 8 bits from the specified I/O port.

procedure oport(**int** port.number,data)
! write the bottom 8 bits of 'data' to the I/O port.

procedure pwr(**real** x,y -> **real**)
! exp(y * ln(x))

procedure random(**int** x -> **int**)
! takes the non zero seed 'x' and produces a non-zero random number
! between -32768 and 32767.

procedure printer(-> **file**)
! returns the file descriptor of the hard copy printer.

procedure idisk(-> **string**)
! returns the disk drive name.

Unix only

procedure exec(***string**)
! execute a Unix process.

procedure fork(-> **int**)
! fork a Unix process and return the child ID.

procedure wait(**int** n -> ***int**)
! wait for a Unix process.

VMS only

procedure find.substr(**string** target,substring -> **int**)
! return the starting position of string 'sub.string'
! in 'target', zero otherwise.

procedure trap.ctrlC(-> **bool**)
! return whether control C has been pressed since the last
! call of this procedure or the start of the program.

procedure date(-> **string**)
! gives the date

procedure time(-> **string**)
! returns the CPU time used since logging in.

INDEX

Only initial references and subsequent important recurrences are listed. Quite frequently references are continued on subsequent pages. Some commonly used symbols are listed at the end of the index.

abort	69	boolean negation	68
abs	26,175	boolean variable	39
abstraction, principle of	148	b.or	177
abstractions	157	braces	21
abstract picture	134	bubblesort	55
access.mode	99	**by**	20,136
Adamson	162		
Algol S	148	call by value	80,158
Algol W	148,151	cartesian point	135
Algol 60	148	**case**	59
Algol 68	148	character order	43
and	37,68	**cint**	53,68
apostrophe	2	cint, creal, etc	68
ASCII	43,173	circle	144
atan	175	code	44,175
		colour	137
′b	66	combine pictures	135
backspace	66	comment	15,71
backtrack	120	compiler directive	71
b.and	177	concatenation	41,155
BCPL	156	conceptual store	151
begin	21	concrete syntax	153,159
bool	68	condition	23
Boole	69	constancy	156
boolean	23,37,154	constant	11,26
boolean connectives	68	constant vector	49,55

control structures	157	find.substr	178
cos	175	flush	100
CP/M	98,177	**for**	19
create file	98	fork	177
		formal parameter	76
data	21	**forward** declaration	84
data structure	48	French verbs	62
data type	178	**from**	137
date	178	function	69
Davie	162	function parameter	108
declarations	158,165		
decode	44,175	gcd	35
default	60	generic type	164
design philosophy	147	gformat	176
Desjardins	148	graphics	134
dictionary order	38,42,56	Gunn	157
digit function	44,176		
Dijkstra	148,149	Habberman	148
directives	71	heuristic	120,130
div	5	Hilbert curve	141
division operator	4	Hoare	148,151
do	19,32	hyper rules	164,169
Donahue	151		
dotted line	140	identifier	162
double integral	109	idisk	177
draw	138	**if do**	32,157
		if then else	34,157
eformat	47,176	iformat	176
eight queens	131	**in**	137
element	48,51	index list	70
ellipse	146	initialising declaration	11
else	34	I/O models	153,159
empty string	43	**int**	53,68
end	21	integer	154
end of file	25	integer expression	3
eof	25,102	integer literal	1
epsilon	70	integer width	33,66
erase.to	137	iport	177
exec	177	**is**	92
exp	175	**isnt**	92
		ISWIM	147
factorial	19	i.w	67,70
false	23		
fformat	67,176	join	135
fibonacci	33,38,79		
fiddle.r	177	knight's tour	124
field	89	Knuth	158
file	25,98,154,159		
file descriptor	98	Landin	147,149
file.name	99	Lecarme	148

Ledgard	152,157	out.byte	102
length	41,69,155,176	outline	134
let	11	**output**	67
letter	44,176	outputsize	66
Lindsay	153	overprint	66
linear list	48		
line.number	175	'p	66
linked list	95	parameter	76,158
LISP	147	parameterless procedure	77
Liskov	150	Pascal	150,151,155,156
list of expressions	3	**peek**	101
list of structures	95	pi	12,70
%list	71	**pic**	134
ln	175	PL360	147
local name	75	plot	177
loop	23	**pntr**	88,163
lower bound	53	***pntr**	88
L-value	156	point order	135
lwb	55	polynomial	79
		principle of	
Marcotty	152	abstraction	150,161
maxint	70	correspondence	149,161
maxreal	70	data type completeness	150,161
McCarthy	147	printer	177
meta rules	164,169	priorities	68
meta symbol	163	**procedure**	74
multiplication operator	3	procedure	
mutual recursion	82	body	75
		call	75
'n	66	heading	160
name	13,75,158	type	164
Naur	148	value	78
von Neumann	155	productions	162
new line	7,66,81		
new page	66	quadratic	61
Newton	26	question mark	2
nil	88	quicksort	112,116
%nolist	71	Quine	151
not	25	quotes	1
%noul	71		
nullfile	99	rabs	26,176
		random	177
'o	66	range of vector	49
object	48	read	86,101
of	48,53,59	read.a.line	101
open file	98	readb	101
operator priorities	68	read.byte	102
options	176	readi	10,11,101
oport	177	readr	11,101
or	37,68	reads	11,101

real	12,68,154	store protection	156
real constant	26	store update	148
real width	66	Strachey	150,156
recursion	95,111	**string**	41,68,154
recursive	82,121	string constant	41
references	167	string variable	42
relational operators	68,92	**structure**	87,155
relative files	100	structure	
rem	5	field	88
repeat	26,157	instance	87
repeat while	27	type	164
repeat while do	27	subscript	48
reserved word	2,176	substring	42,155
reverse list	96	symmetric order	95
reverse string	45	syntax	162,169
rotate	136	syntactic category	162
Rouse Ball	110	s.w	67,70
r.w	67,70		
		't	66
S-algol program	164	table	48
SASL	147	tabulate	66
scalar data type	154,163	Tennent	148
scale	136	**text**	137
Schumann	153	**then**	34
scope	22,28,160	time	178
scrn.x.max	138	%title	71
scrn.y.max	138	**to**	19,137
scrn.x.min	138	top down	74
scrn.y.min	138	Towers of Hanoi	95,110
seek	100	trap.ctrlC	178
semicolon	15,70	trapezoidal rule	108
sequence of clauses	21	tree sort	93
shift	136	triangular vector	53
shift.l	176	**true**	23
shift.r	176	truncate	106,175
Sieve of Eratosthenes	106,116	Turner	147
simple data type	68	type checking	148
sin	175	type void	164
s.i	70,101		
sort	50,52,55,93	%ul	71
sort tree	93	underline	71
s.o	70,101	UNIX	98,177
spaces	67	**upb**	55
special characters	66	upper bound	53
square root	26,61		
sqrt	61,69,175	value, call by	80,158
standard function	175	VAX/VMS	98,178
standard identifier	70	**vector**	48,155,163
store	148,153	constant	49
store constancy	156	declaration	48

initialisation	48
limits	51
of vectors	51
range	49
type	48
void	164
void clause	165
wait	177
while do	23
van Wijngaarden	148,149,162
Wirth	147,154
write	1,66
!	15,71
%	71
&	135
'	66
"	2
'n	7
*	3,54
++	41
,	3,51
->	78
/	4
:	59,67
::	48
::=	163
:=	13
;	15
=	11
?	1,164
@	53
[ ]	53
^	135
~	25
{ }	21,162
|	42,162